Tiger Guide

TO

"INFORMATION SECURITY"

Tiger Guide

TO

"INFORMATION SECURITY"

SHAWN ROHRBACH, M.F.A.

Golden Bear Publishers

2007

ISBN: 978-1-4276-2524-3

Published by Golden Bear Publishers

About the Author

Shawn Rohrbach earned his BA in Philosophy from the Seminary of Christ the King in Mission, British Columbia, Canada. He studied Information Systems in the MBA/Information Technology program at City University in Bellevue, Washington. He earned his Master of Fine Arts at Naropa University in Boulder Colorado. He is currently working as a staff information technology consultant at San Diego State University. He is an avid cyclist, skier, rock climber and has recently taken up boogie boarding.

Note from the Publisher

The Tiger Guide to Information Security is a well-written guide that covers areas of information security provides essential information about a topic that is without doubt on the minds of anyone who has questions about the security of computers in general and more specifically the information computers contain and how to protect it.

Author, Shawn Rohrbach, discusses, in great detail, common issues that network administrators face each day and also poses numerous solutions to problems that face information security personnel. With valuable step-by-step analysis, definitely valuable material for anyone involved with Information Technology, private business persons, public network administrators, government contractors and anyone who simply wants to understand how to prevent problems that arise with computers.

This is a great Tiger Guide and a very valuable source of information for anyone with interest in computers and information security.

Thank you for buying our Tiger Guide to Information Security.

Sincerely,

William M. Frantz, M.B.A., J.D.

President, Golden Bear Publishers

Contents

Introduction to Information Security Assurance

Imagine a day in the United States when no one could access their money through an ATM. Millions of people would rush to the bank branches to withdraw money Imagine further if the tellers could not issue any money because their computers were down. People would probably take whatever cash they had on hand and try to pump gas from computerized gas pumps or to purchase food from stores using automated cash registers, and would get nothing.

This scenario is real and was played out in the 2005 hurricane Katrina suffered throughout Southern Louisiana and Mississippi. The cause of this system wide shut down was not a computer hacker in a dark basement, it was an environmental hazard.

Even small businesses that were not flooded during hurricane Katrina were not functional as long as there was no electricity to operate their computers. In most areas of the southern delta, this problem persisted for weeks and even months. If a company was lucky enough to avoid the flooding, they still lost money and could not access essential data. For those who were flooded, they understood immediately the value of secure off site storage of data.

Following the attack on the World Trade Center in 2001, several large and small companies were ready to resume operations the following week because of astute planning. These plans included both back up of all data as well as redundant systems deployed in obscure locations allowing them to re-locate personnel, restore data from back up, establish and test telecommunications and resume business. Those who had not planned for catastrophe or for potential mitigation took months and even years to completely restore operations. Natural disasters are often overlooked as the cause of network failure.

Consider also the fate of an IT administrator for a very large East Coast University. He served time in a federal prison because as the primary administrator of Information Systems, he was aware of the flagrant use of the network to download and sell illegal copies of popular software programs. Not only did he not prevent the activity, he gained financially from it. A network administrator for a business located in the Seattle area was sent to prison for not reporting and participating in an investigation of child pornography that was stored on his server, and he was not the person who downloaded the pictures. Illicit and illegal use of network resources is a costly risk.

The very large Wide Area Networks (WANs) that support the likes of Proctor and Gamble, Microsoft, Exxon, GM, General Electric and Bank of America are a few hundred in total count. There are also large networks serving major universities and through Internet2, these are further inter-networked. However, there are thousands of smaller but equally important computer networks supporting the majority of small home based and business networks, and they are always the most vulnerable to risk.

The focus of this Guide is to understand the common risks, develop systems and policies for analyzing the potential for any given risk and to take specific, practical action to prevent and mitigate them. To properly cover this subject, we need to study both the underlying technologies as well as the practical methods for securing small networks.

The book focuses on two levels of network security from the very basic concepts and methods right through advanced concepts including hardening operating systems, applying encryption and designing redundant systems. The goal is to offer the information in a manner that anyone can understand and use. For each topic presented, there is a theoretical explanation of the underlying technologies and the potential vulnerabilities. The reader will then be guided through a process of analyzing if their systems are at risk. This guide book will offer an explanation of the technology underlying various security issues as well as the theory behind the application of security measures. The combination of a clear understanding of the technology of networking along with the theory of securing it will enable the reader to develop their own security strategies for their unique needs. I do not rely on vendor base solutions. These are usually packaged and do little to help the owner understand why certain security measures need to be applied. The 'how' of security is easy if the reader understands the 'why'? I believe everyone who operates a computer can and should be able to safely secure their systems and data.

This guidebook culminates in specific information about applying these theories to securing systems intending to support the business needs of defense contractors. It will become clear as the reader works through the various levels of security theory that the requirements of the Department of Defense for securing data pertinent to national security are founded on solid principles of information security.

This guide is intended to build on concepts, starting with basic security concepts and ending with more complex theories that rely on an understanding of the basic building blocks. There is also an underlying assumption through out this book that we should be concerned more about security threats originating from within the system, and not as conventional wisdom tells use, from outside. Outside threats are real and are handily dealt with as we will see. The internal security threats need to be addressed directly and my experience tells me most organizations are not responding well enough to this issue.

One final thought on security. It will become evident that I prioritize security in this order.

1) People

2) Data

3) Systems

4) Infrastructure

While this flies a little in the face of some security theory, it will always remain my focus.

Security =
1) People +
2) Data; +
3) Systems +
4) Infrastructure

Level I

Computer Networking Technologies and Common Risks

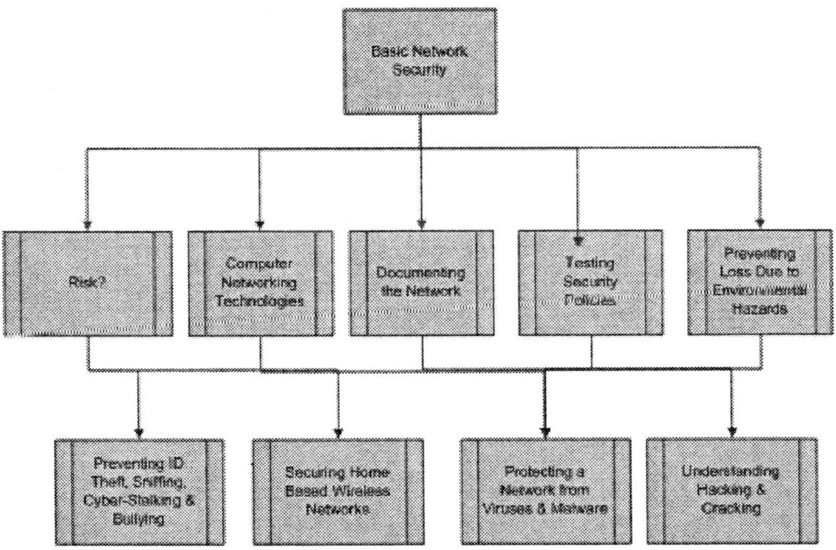

Chapter 1

What is at Risk?

Chapter Objectives

- Analyzing what is at risk when processing or storing electronic information
- Four basic loss risks:
    - ✓ Physical Security
    - ✓ Connectivity
    - ✓ Hardware and Software
    - ✓ Data
- Analyzes loss due to hardware failure
- Analyzes loss due to environmental catastrophes
- Analyzes loss due to human intervention

In order to fully understand the process of securing electronic information, we need to focus on what is at risk. What could the crackers, user error and natural disasters do to our computer networks? Too often some potential targets are overlooked until it is too late or computer users focus on only one or two types of potential loss.

There are four basic categories of loss.

- **Physical Security** that could result in death or physical harm to human beings or destruction of company assets.
- **Connectivity** of our network with other networks thereby suspending normal business operations
- **Hardware and Software Infrastructure** that supports our Information Systems could fail for any number of reasons.
- Loss of **Data** of all types that would potentially suspend operations, reveal personal and financial information or result ion the loss of intellectual property.

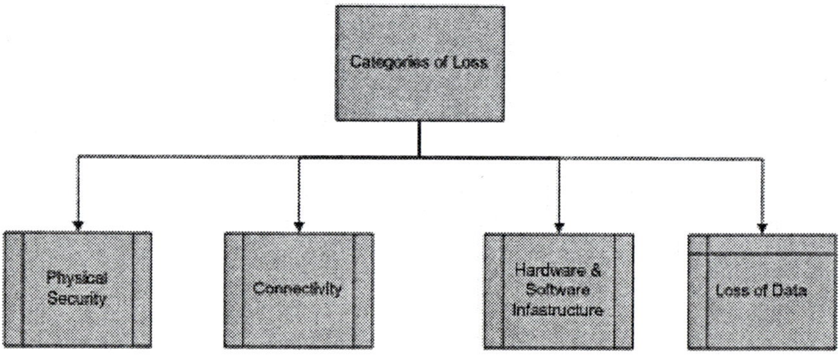

Each loss can be represented by a dollar value which is the outcome of a thorough risk analysis. Our focus in this chapter is to analyze specifically what could be lost and how this might affect people and business operations.

Physical Security

In preparing for the CISSP ™, we learn a valuable lesson early on. A question is asked about a scenario where there is imminent physical danger and you are the network administrator. You are to decide what you must save first from a list of very important networking objects. One of these choices is people. The correct answer is always save the people first, then get to the server, data tapes or whatever else might be the next most important object.

Threats to human life as a result of intentional or accidental failure of computer systems are rare, but they occur frequently enough to be a concern of any network security analyst.

A convict escaped from a local jail in our area last summer. As soon as he was free and in the proximity of persons who testified against him, he set out to murder them. In analyzing the jail break, it was determined the software used to automate locks had failed momentarily and the convict took the opportunity to walk out the back service entrance to the jail. An astute police officer was successful in identifying the convict and he was recaptured before he could inflict harm.

In September of 2004, the computers in the air traffic control systems serving mostly California but directly affecting the entire west coast failed. There was no automated air traffic control available for the west coast for several hours and the potential danger of commercial jets attempting to use the same air space or runway was very real. The debate continues today as to whether this was human error or operating system failure. Regardless of the outcome of the debate, the failure was within the computerized system.

In May of 2005, the computerized tram system in Manchester England suffered a system wide software failure. The result was a complete cessation of tram service as the drivers had no way of piloting the trams safely. All operations ceased due to concern for the safety of passengers.

In New York, a father was able to locate the day care his child was enrolled in through the internet. A careless web master allowed photographs of children on a field trip to be published. After some searching, the father found the site and was able to then track his child's movements. He abducted his son in spite of the mother's best efforts to keep the location of the day care secret.

Other than causing eventual degradation of eyesight or carpel-tunnel syndrome, computer systems do not directly threaten human life. The threats are typically a consequence of the actual system failure, but they are real.

Systems that are computerized and designed to protect human life are rarely monitored as closely as systems housing mission critical data. Information about people who could be threatened is often accessible through the internet. We will discuss later in this book systems and policies that will mitigate this risk. It will be noted that the primary concern of any security plan will be first to protect human life.

Connectivity

Students of Information Technology are often confronted with a confusing array of definitions for Quality of Service, (QoS). Some network engineers define it as the percentage of time their server operates without requiring a reboot. This is one very small aspect of the concept of QoS. More precisely QoS refers to the quality of the connectivity a system has with other networked systems or the Internet in general, as well as how the data that needs to migrate is queued. Qos is comprised of both the connectivity and the hierarchy of data which then ensures the proper transfer. The primary concern is the connection. Without connectivity between systems or to the Internet, data cannot be moved.

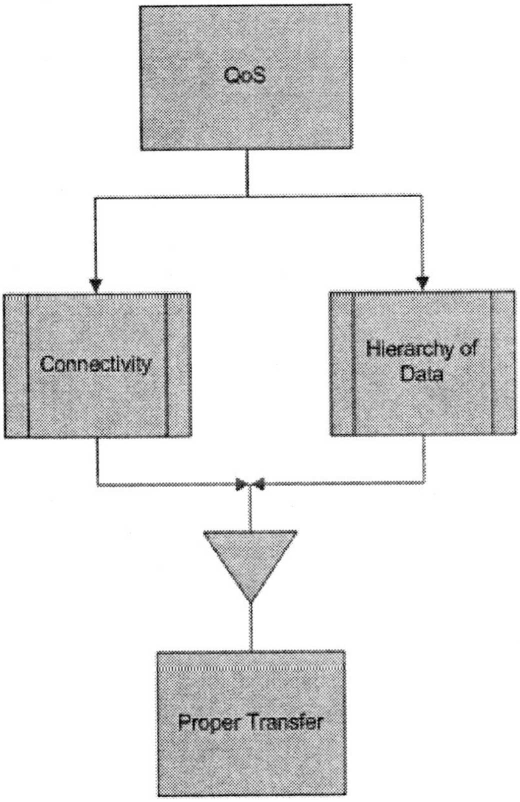

Not every disruption of connectivity is a threat to normal operations; Internet Service Providers (ISP) disrupts their own service from time to time for system maintenance and upgrades. Some providers do a better job than others of informing customers of the outage. Sometimes the customer just has to understand the internet is down and will come back up when the provider finishes the task or finds the failed link in the system.

Malicious disruption of internet connectivity is not as common as technical failures; however it does occur frequently enough to be a major concern. Worm viruses are written specifically to disrupt internet connectivity by flooding servers and workstations until they cannot function and the connectivity is lost. Worse than this, however, is the student who accessed the ceiling above a server room and simply cut the T-1 line. This event actually happened in Denver and the local phone company, Internet Service Provider and school network administrators scratched their heads for a while and after testing the cable physically traced the cable to the cut. The company who originally ran the T-1 cable for the school was called on an emergency basis to run a new cable. Internet service was re-established for the school the next day and the student who cut the cable was never caught.

More common than malicious disruption of connectivity is disruption as a result of old or incompatible connection hardware. The relationship between national ISPs and local telecom companies in an era of deregulation is often a complex one. Frequently the end user is prevented from contacting the local telecom company and any problems with local connections must be dealt with by the ISP. This can result in very frustrating service calls where the local telecom technicians will test continuity of a line, but do not run data tests through sometimes arcane connections. With the rise of M PLS over VPN as a fast and secure protocol for transferring sensitive data, local telecoms are finding their equipment was not designed to recognize and therefore handle these protocols. The result is termed a ***circuit flap***. Data is transmitted through the local connection and as the equipment analyzes the protocols and does not recognize them, the circuit fails and the connection is lost.

Other than old equipment not recognizing new protocols, another cause in the disruption of connectivity can be in the routing tables that either end of the Wide Area Network (WAN). Data is routed by IP and Media Access Control (MAC) addressing. If two different people set up the routers, it is not uncommon for them to be configured differently. This will result in something that appears like a circuit flap, but the result is the same; loss of connectivity.

Troubleshooting this type of failure requires more than simple circuit tests. Continuity can be established and maintained, yet it will appear that there is not connectivity. More complex tests must be run to analyze the packets and frames going through the local and national telecom connections. Fluke created analytical tools such as the **Optiiview** ™ and other network analyzers that do more than simply test continuity. The price of these network analyzers may prevent most administrators from owning them, but several network security consultants and network hardware rental firms make them available for short term projects at reasonable cost.

Later in this guide we will discuss policies and methods that will mitigate and respond to loss of connectivity. To properly effect these policies and mitigation plans it is necessary to spend time learning about the relationship your ISP has with the local telecom companies that serve your local or national WANs. It's not your Plain Old Telephone System (POTS) anymore.

Hardware Infrastructure

It is not easy but also not impossible for hardware infrastructure to suffer from an external attack outside of your company walls. The closest to this I have observed was a program written by a man in response to the problem of trafficking illegal pornography. His program actually caused the hardware within a Central Processing Unit (CPU) to fail. He could attack the post, the bios, the hard drive and even the power supply. He then found persons who thought they were going to receive some illegal pornographic images but instead downloaded his program. The result was hardware failure. I do not recommend this course of action to anyone and in fact it is illegal no matter how much we may support this father's efforts.

The more typical examples of hardware failure fall into three categories.

- **Mechanical Failure**
- **Failure cause by Human Intervention**
- **Failure caused by Environmental Hazards.**

Mechanical Failures

Simple Mechanical Failure involves hard drives, motherboards, power supplies, UPS systems failures and cd-rom or flash memory failure. These are mechanical in nature and will all fail eventually. Hard drives on servers are as prone to failure as any home system. In fact, when various computer makers experimented with "hot swap", the ability to pull and replace hard drives, memory, SCSI cards while the computer was running, proved to cause more hardware failure.

Data can be recovered from any hard drive that fails mechanically, but this is not easy or cheap. Good forensics specialists can dig hard drives out of swamps, completely dismantled, and still recover data. However, once a system fails for any of the causes noted above, the system is non-functional until the hardware is replaced or repaired.

This sounds obvious and even suggests obvious solutions for mitigation, perhaps even buying redundant hardware that can quickly replace the failed systems immediately. However, to convince management of the necessity of redundant hardware when they are looking at a brand new blade server just out of the box is not as easy as it sounds.

It is difficult to predict normal mechanical failure. Some users brag about hardware lasting almost by the decade, while others buy a lap top computer only to see it in the shop most of the time. What cannot be avoided is these two truths: 1) Hardware will fail eventually and 2) The computer network is most likely non-functional until the hardware is replaced.

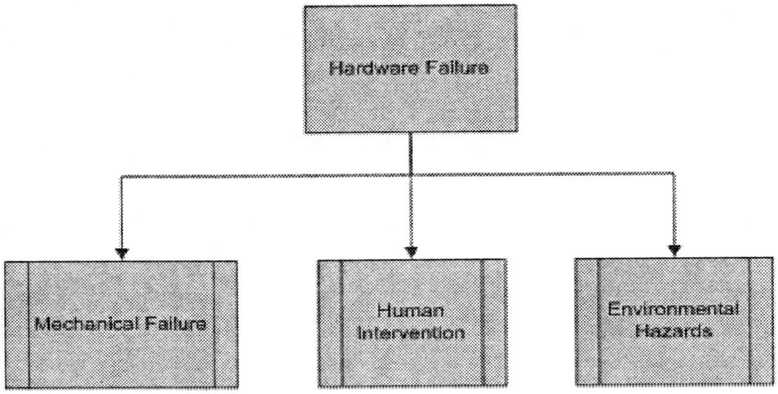

Failure caused by Human Intervention

Intentional damage of hardware by an internal perpetrator is more common than we would like to admit. In one proprietary school where I consulted, the outgoing systems administrator became too friendly with two technical students. These students knew how to cause hardware failure and once they had access to the server room, perpetrated a crime involving ten thousand dollars worth of hardware and then an unknown dollar figure attached to lost productivity when they poured water into the servers, routers and switches.

Equally destructive and more easily preventable are the hazards of food and beverages causing hardware failure. I was network administrator in a small multimedia company and over a period of one year I replaced twenty keyboards, five mother boards and ten power supplies as a result of employees enjoying coffee, snacks, lunch, late night pizza and beer at their workstations.

Hardware failure caused by human intervention, whether by simple negligence or intentional malice, is far more common than simple mechanical failure. Mitigating this will be dealt with later in this guide.

Failure caused by Environmental Hazards

The loss of computer and network services due to environmental hazards is common and is not limited to catastrophic events. As noted above, a server room without proper air condition can cause hardware and there for complete system failure. A false fire alarm in a water based system can cause hardware failure and also complete system failure. I want to divide this section two ways. First, there are the obvious

Environmental Catastrophies such as earthquakes, hurricanes, tornados, floods, fires and the like. Second, there are hazards caused by less **Minor Catastrophic Phenomenon** like dust, heat, fire prevention, improper loading of shelves and computer racks and simple carelessness.

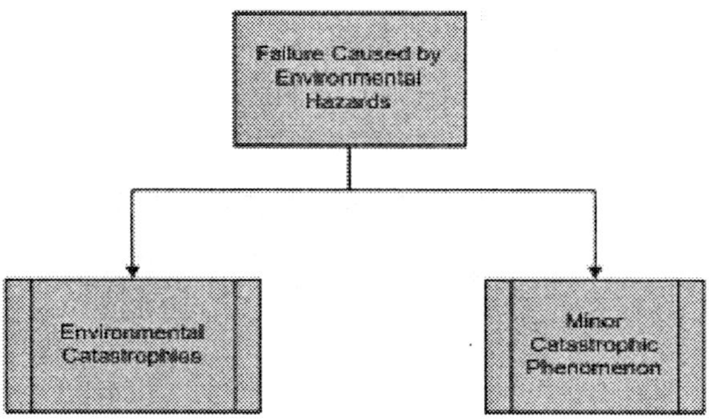

Environmental Catastrophies.

When the dust settled from the attacks on 9/11, there was first the count of human lives lost in this attack. After this, companies assessed the damage to their Information System Infrastructures. No one spent time salvaging hard drives and back up tapes once the human count was finished; the trucks came in and started hauling away the debris. If the hard drives in use in the two towers had valuable information, the only recovery would have been that information that had been backed up and stored off site.

During and after the Hurricane Katrina, rescuers spent their time saving lives and recovering bodies; they spent no time trying to recover hard drives, back up tapes and computer systems. If the systems were not backed up prior to the storm and flooding, the data was lost and whole systems serving banks, insurance companies, schools and hospitals were completely inoperable.

(Aftermath of Katrina)

In part of Indonesia following the Sunami of December 2004, villages had struggled for years to build computing services only to see them wiped out completely by the water. A year after the event, if these villages even exist, the computing systems had not yet been replaced.

In large catastrophic events where there is the risk of or actual loss of human life, the primary focus must be on protecting human life or recovering the dead. Computer systems are quite correctly not of any concern until this task is completed. There is almost no way of preventing many of these large events, but there are strategies for mitigating damage to computer systems which will be discussed later in this book. Part of that mitigation plan should be a plan for rapid recovery and restoration of all Information Systems.

Minor Catastrophic Phenomenon

In a small investment company with one central office and five satellite offices, a disgruntled system administrator had been seeking approval for air conditioning in the server room for two years, claiming the heat generated by the serves was going to cause catastrophic system failure. He is correct; prolonged exposure to heat can causes system boards to fail. He decided, however, to elevate the urgency of his dire predictions and sealed the server room from any ventilation, turned on a propane heater and caused the heat to rise to over one hundred and twenty +degrees. The resulting failure was as predicted; mother boards, circuits, memory and eventually the hard drives failed and then he quit his job.

One of my major concerns as the administrator of a heavily accessed system has been carelessness with food and beverages. Keyboards are usually the first to go as soda, coffee, cookie crumbs and ice cream spill out of their containers. And, yes, a motherboard can be easily ruined when liquids are poured on it. Later in this book, we will discuss the importance of policies that clearly address this issue. The concept is fairly easy; a desk is for work, a dining table is for eating.

While an overheated room and sloppy employees are not viewed as the most important threat to a networking system, more time is spent by network administrators mitigating or repairing network problems because of these seemingly insignificant actions.

Data Loss and Identity Theft

Data can be lost, destroyed or stolen. Sensitive data containing trade secrets, operational information, personal records can all be used for financial gain or simply to destroy as much of someone's life or business as possible. This is particularly important in an environment that handles sensitive defense or government information. We will focus specifically in Chapter 12 on how compliance to NISP standards helps network administrators to protect student privacy and the integrity of their data.

There are a variety of methods for gaining access to data. Typically we think data is most vulnerable to hackers who access our system remotely and steal or destroy. The truth is most networks are fairly well protected at the perimeter using a variety of routing techniques, firewalls, fireboxes all within a secure architecture. We will cover this in more detail later in this book. My experience of data that is lost, stolen or destroyed has clearly proven it is usually caused by internal personnel. This can be both accidental as well as malicious. There is a genuine fear among those who know this well a terrorist will have better luck stealing data if they have a job in the company they want to steal from.

As an experiment t, I parked outside the office of a large regional bank with a laptop outfitted with inexpensive software used to "sniff" chat sessions. Most Instant Messaging services use the same protocols and the same ports. Data in the chat sessions migrates across the wired or wireless network as plain text. In simple terms, anyone with the forty dollar chant sniffing software can easily intercept any and all chats that are taking place on and given network.

I had warned the managers of this bank that I knew of people who had intercepted their chats, and quite innocently by accident. They did not express much concern over this; that is until I handed them a print out of five chats sessions taking place between employees and customers regarding commercial loans. The print outs contained extremely private information including contact phone numbers, social security number, bank account information and more.

The managers immediately directed employees to stop using all forms of Instant Messaging until they could encrypt the data and formulate new policies that would ensure the safe use of this communication tool.

Sniffing chats is not the only problem with most Instant Messaging services. The protocol most typically used, H.323, allows sessions to remain opened on the default port. Two people may be in a session, but are not typing information. The ports on both ends are in a receptive mode and are not shielded from receiving any kind of data, especially viruses and spyware. Rather than having to bother with the effort to encrypt data and secure ports, most corporate IT personnel simply request policies forbidding the use of Instant Messaging of any kind.

A network administrator for a large, multi-location corporation was mandated to conduct regular back ups and to have those back up tapes stored securely off site. The corporation retained the services of a company that routinely picked up data storage tapes and stored them in underground vaults. The driver of this company was required to report the number of tapes picked up at each location and consistently reported no tapes from this one location. An auditor was sent to review the log books and to visit the network administrator. The auditor found nine hundred back up tapes in boxes in the basement of the facility. A rain storm had caused the drainage to overflow and most of the tapes had been submerged under water until the drain was cleared. This obviously destroyed all of the data.

As we proceed, we now know what can be lost. Let's look next at the basic technologies of computer networking so we can properly plan for security.

Chapter 2
Understanding Network Technology

Chapter Objectives

- Understanding Binary and Computer Functions
- Understanding Data Transmission
- Data Transmission, Packets and Network Addressing
- Basic concepts in data storage, preservation and corruption
- Basic concepts in Internet Architecture

In spite of many attempts by computer specialists to make networking technology seem complicated, it is really easy to understand. For the purposes of this guide, we will focus on how data, whether it is email, Word documents, photographs or video, is created, transmitted and viewed. This will help us understand the subsequent issues pertaining to network security.

Data Creation

Let's start with the creation of data. Computer programs are designed to make it easy to write a letter, retouch a digital photograph or send an email. We see the actual document, photograph or video as the recipient will see it. However, for the data to be stored or transmitted, it must be converted to something that low voltage electricity can deal with and that is what is known as binary, one or zero. The hard drive in the computer or the fancy flash drive people carry on straps around their necks can only see these patterns of ones and zeros. Computer programs, when instructed, search for specific patterns and re-produce them on the monitor or send them to the printer and we have a hard copy of what was once nothing more than electronic impulses.

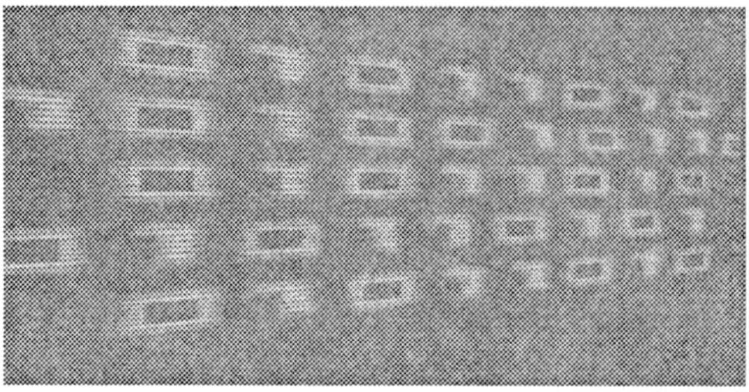

It is the patterns of the ones and zeros that is most interesting to me and is the focus of this book. Every letter in the alphabet, every number and every symbol on a computer keyboard has a specific pattern of ones and zeros. Each one or zero is a bit, and eight of these in a specific pattern are called a byte. The word "dog" therefore has twenty four bits or three bytes, each one or zero in the byte patterned to represent the letters D, O and G. A word processing software program will read these patterns and produce the word "dog" on the screen.

Old school programmers once wrote software applications using binary. They had memorized the some 250 different binary representations of letters, numbers and symbols. Subsequent programmers were given tools to program called compilers. They could write programs in a way that represented their speaking language and the compiler would convert this to binary and store it on the hard drive. As well, someone can use a digital camera to take a picture of a birthday party. The picture is always patterns of ones or zeros until it is sent to a printer and it becomes a hard copy photograph.

Basis of Computer Networking

The basis of all computer networking then remains conversion from common language or visual representation to patterns of ones and zeros, transmitting these ones and zeros using low voltage electricity and then re-assembling them in the recipient computer for viewing, printing or storage.

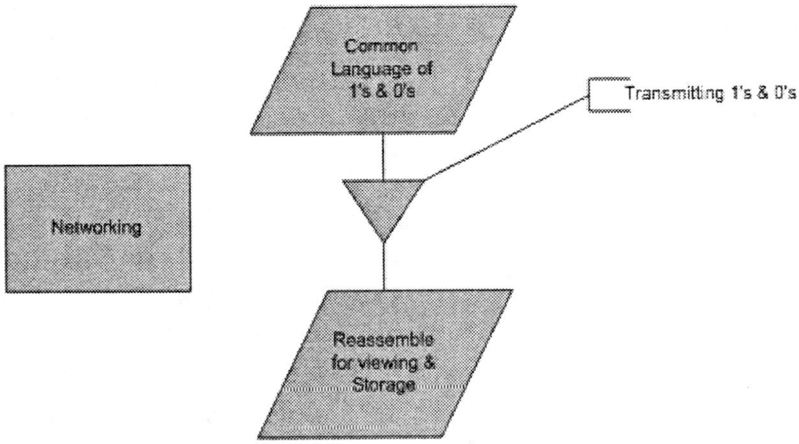

Low voltage electricity can pass through a wide variety of mediums. Typically, it passes through thin copper wire whether it is telephone wire or what is known as Cat 5, a wire typically used for computer networks. It is fun to demonstrate that low voltage electricity can also pass through glass tubes (commonly known as fiber optics), copper pipes, barbed wire and anything else that allows conductivity. Data, or electronic impulses that are read as on or off (ones or zeros) can safely pass through anything that allows conductivity. It is useful to point out here this is always a concern for network security personnel; data that is passing with low voltage electricity can pass through almost anything and can also be easily diverted or viewed as it passes. If a word processing program created the document, the same word processing program can open the document and read it. The document can also be opened and read by other programs. This is the first concern in computer network security.

Data Distribution

The next concept to understand is how data is distributed. Computer networking was developed to deliver data accurately. There is nothing useful about a system that delivers inaccurate or partial data. All of the data must be reproduced by another computer exactly they way the writer or photographer intended it to be seen.

Low voltage electricity passing through copper wire can carry only small amounts of data at any given time. This amounts to about one page of written material. Fiber Optic and Cable can carry slightly larger amounts of data in one segment. Let's say I want to send my most recent mystery novel to an unsuspecting editor who will be thrilled to receive it in his morning email. My novel is one thousand three hundred pages long and has a surprise ending. I need to break this novel down into about one thousand three hundred different segments of ones and zeros and then have it reassemble as the editor anxiously opens his email and finds my delightful novel.

Computer programs know this and are written to divide data into what is known as packets or frames, the difference between them not important at this time. What is important is the mechanism used to organize the packets or frames so they reassemble correctly at the recipient computer. Each packet is tagged with a number so the one thousand three hundred packets of my novel reassemble correctly so I can get the contract on my book. The packet also carries two other types of information to ensure my novel arrives at the editor's desk and not my arch rival novelist who wants to steal my ideas.

This system was developed by several different scientists and was partially funded by the defense department who wanted a computerized system for things like sending commands to nuclear weapons. The system was designed to be accurate. The command was going to be sent from one point and then to another exact point, such as a missile silo. Sending the command to every computer in the world and hoping the right computer would read it was completely unacceptable. The additional data is an addressing system that identifies the network the computer is on and then the exact computers that are the sender and the recipient. It is the same concept as old snail mail; write the correct address on the envelope and the letter will most likely arrive at the correct address.

Addresses

> The first address is an Internet Protocol (IP) address and the second in a Media Access Control (MAC) address. The IP address identifies the network and locates the computer. The MAC address specifically identifies the computer.

For those who are reading and wondering how law enforcement knows who is sending what data, especially illegal data, this is the basis of that investigative work. These addresses might change for any number of reasons, but the history of the activity is permanently archived in computer network systems. It never goes away. I spent some time in my life archiving data and addresses for email that was sent through an Internet Service Provider (ISP). Most of it was pure dribble, but occasionally it was taken as evidence of illegal activity on the internet and the history of that activity was permanently preserved and the result was a rightful conviction.

The key principle is simple; computer networks were invented to be precise, not private. This is the second important concept to understand in reference to network security.

Data Storage

Next, let's look at the storage of data. Going back to the Preface of this book where I alluded to the Katrina hurricane, the total loss of information assets and resources was not limited to computers submerged under water. Legal, financial and other types of data were permanently lost.

Bank records reflecting savings, checking and investment accounts were gone. If there were no duplicated copies of this data in storage, these records were lost permanently.

Data is stored in the one and zero format in various ways. It could be stored on a metallic hard drive disk, metallic tape and now even in glass. Of greatest concern is the integrity of the data; that is it is the data and exactly the data that was intended to be stored. In reference to the emails I archived, all of the data associated with those emails must be properly in tact or it is not evidence. As well, when I agree to work somewhere, the data regarding my pay checks must be exactly what we agreed on. If I am paid too much, then I should report that and certainly if I am paid too little, I will definitely report it. In either case, the data regarding my pay check was not accurate.

Data is also valuable to competing businesses, insurance companies, credit card companies, thieves and mom. Data should be available only to the people who need to or have a right to know the information. The data regarding AIDS patients in any given city would be of interest to an insurance company, but they should have access only when it is their legitimate right to do so. Mom might be very interested in her college aged son's attendance and grades, but by law she does not have the right to access it until her son gives her that right. Data must be Confidential.

Finally, data should be Available. Systems should be in place that will respect the Integrity of the data, keep it confidential but also make it available to legitimate users. Later in this book when we examine securing information for Department of Defense (DoD) contracting, these same needs will be very important to consider and it is good for us to cover them now in a different context.

Permanently destroying data is one way to corrupt it. The company can assume I never existed and not pay me at all. Improperly entering the data can corrupt it. Adding another zero to my salary looks good to me, but it's not what the company agreed to pay me. My nephew, who is fairly good with computers, could attempt to access the data and add the zero illicitly and hope I would share the new found wealth with him. This kind of data corruption usually gets all the attention and will be handled in good time in this guide.

The reality is simple; data is never permanently destroyed. People think that "deleting" a file really means permanently removing the file from a storage medium such as a hard or flash drive. The file is only masked and the computer is told to write data over the deleted data. The old data remains. Software applications have been written to identify data that has been over written, look for patterns of ones and zeros and then reproduce the "deleted" data. As a demonstration, I used to have students "delete a file, then disassemble the hard drive, throw the hard drive disks in water and leave them over night. In the morning, I would dry the disk, reassemble the hard drive and find then find and display the deleted file. If I sell or recycle a computer, I remove the hard drive, remove the disk from the hard drive case, destroy the disks with a hammer and properly dispose of the shattered disk according to local law. Then the data is permanently destroyed.

Permanent destruction of data stored on a typical hard drive is difficult, but not impossible. Recovery of the data requires very expensive software. Data stored on magnetic tape is easily destroyed. The tape can easily be burned, cut, overheated or soaked in water and the magnetic qualities are lost along with the data. But this is not my primary concern when I think of safely storing data.

Data Entry

Data entry is a flawed process. When I was in high school, the army was convinced I was a female and hotly recruited me to join as a woman. Someone simply entered my name into the arcane computer and selected "female" when they were required to identify my sex. There is an old, well worn expression that refers to this as GIGO, Garbage In, Garbage Out. Even the most current scanning hardware and software make mistakes and misidentify letters, numbers and characters and the data is corrupted. The computer will accept as true any keystroke you enter, no matter how badly the word or number is mangled.

Data is only as good at the method of transferring it to a digital format and the media on which it is stored. Many long discussions focus on data security and they are simple in principle; enter the data correctly and choose a media that will survive the natural destruction caused by exposure to elements or disasters.

The approach I have taken in this chapter is to look at the essential elements of data without getting lost in some of the complexities of specific data processing. Computers deal with data in a manner that allows us to see the product, but always manipulates, transmits and stores it in binary form. These ones and zeros are transmitted to exact locations using addresses and low voltage electricity and finally the data is stored in a somewhat permanent fashion as binary.

This may seem simplistic and it really is. Computer networking was designed around the existing telephone infrastructure because twisted copper wire was known to efficiently conduct low voltage electricity and therefore binary data. The invention of the modem, a device that converts digital low voltage to analog low voltage that could be easily transmitted over existing telephone wires was the biggest first step in revolutionizing computer networking and gave birth to the explosion of the internet. The basics of computer networking have not changed even though the medium of transmission over fiber optic and cable allow for faster transmission of larger packets and frames. With this understanding of the essentials of networking technologies, we can successfully proceed to securing a computer network system.

Chapter 3
Documenting a Network

Chapter Objectives

- The need for initial network documentation
- Document now, fix later
- Respond immediately to obvious criminal activity when discovered
- Assess the following areas:
  - ✓ Cabling
  - ✓ Distribution Hardware
  - ✓ Central Processing Units
  - ✓ Networked Peripherals
  - ✓ Physical Security of Data Storage Devices
- Existing Policies

Approaching network security in a disorganized fashion will ultimately result in some form of loss. There is never a guarantee that a tightly organized security plan will prevent all loss, but the odds are substantially better. The best security plan begins with a thorough assessment of the network as it stands.

To complete this assessment effectively, it must be undertaken by someone or a group who has authority to access all areas of the network. Denying access will only result in an incomplete assessment. As a consultant, I have walked away from clients who did not give me total access.

It is also advisable to simply complete the assessment before trying to fix anything. The only exception would be if during the assessment it was discovered someone was actively attempting to illicitly access data or if something illegal was discovered in the process. Laws vary between jurisdictions, but generally proof of fraudulent activity, theft, purposeful destruction of data, storage of illegal pornography and other obviously illegal activities need to be reported immediately to local authorities. Yes, this delays the assessment but to have total access to a system and then to ignore proof of illegal activity places some level of guilt on the assessor.

Aside from reporting illegal activity, this work is not intended to seek out minute problems. This assessment is intended to give administrators a thorough overview of the system. Astute and experienced network administrators will see the obvious flaws in a badly designed system and will be more ready to offer thorough remedies rather than simply patching a system on the fly. Later, an assessment of specific vulnerabilities and performance can be conducted more effectively.

A thorough assessment covers the following areas. Each one will be thoroughly explained as you are guided through the effort of assessing them.

1. Cabling.
2. Distribution Hardware.
3. Central Processing Units (CPUs)
4. Networked Peripherals.
5. Physical Security of Server and Data Storage Devices.
6. Existing Policies.

Cabling

New construction often guarantees state of the art cabling through the structure. Retrofitted office and home improvements makes no guarantee. Cabling is as important as any other aspect of a network and the security of the network relies as much on it as anything else. Recalling the first chapter on determining what is at risk in a network, the actual connectivity and effective delivery of data depends on the quality of the cabling infrastructure.

Starting at the demarcation point, or where the network connection enters the building, we want to follow or test every cable connection to the point where the node plugs in.

Demarcation:

In a small network, the demarcation point can be as simple as where the cable or telephone company has their connection box on the side of the structure. Check for loose or exposed wires. Look for damage to the box used to cover the connections. Look for illicit connections and vampire taps. Someone with a good understanding of electronics can easily tap into a cable or telephone systems to steal cable television and internet service or to monitor the transmission of data. Connections should be clean and obvious. If anything seems out of order and there appears to be connections that are not clearly identified or are loose, call the service responsible for the demarcation connection.

In a larger network, the demarcation point usually is controlled by the local telephone service provider, among them Verizon, Quest and other local service providers. They control access to the lines that are rented by long distance service providers. Typically, a company with multiple locations will contract a national long distance service that might not be with the company who provides local telephone service. Long distance providers contract with the local provider to connect your telephone, dsl, adsl and often fiber optic. Most business parks are not serviced by cable companys. The significance of this is if there is an issue with the cabling, normally a company cannot contact the local provider unless they also provide telephone service. You must contact you long distance provider who rents the lines and they will contact the local company to service the demarcation point.

Now start tracing the cabling from the demarcation point to the first point of distribution, typically in the server room. If this cable is exposed to anyone who wants to see it, you have a problem. A small university lost all internet connectivity when a student cut the cable between the demarcation point and the first distribution point in the server room. Because no one had ever traced the cable, it took several days to find the cut.

Once in the server room, try to determine if the cabling going out to the various nodes are clearly marked. If not, note this. You will want to remedy this later. A well installed cable infrastructure is clearly marked at both ends of the cable in the server room and at the point in the wall where the node connects. This serves the purpose of quickly identifying cabling issues.

I enjoy testing Cat 5 cabling. A line tester costing no more than seventy five dollars and a cheap set of walkie talkies are all you need. The line tester will tell if the cable and RJ45 heads were wired for straight through or cross over throughput. Typically, you want a straight through connection. The tester will tell if there is line interruption such as a cut.

At this point, it is important that a diagram of the cabling infrastructure should be drawn noting the nomenclature of the end points that match in the server room and where the nodes connect. This diagram will be very helpful in the event of loss of service to various nodes or sections.

Cabling from the wall connection to the node should be neatly tucked out of sight, using zip ties or some other connection to secure them together. Loose, sagging or visible cabling from the wall to the node is unsightly and deteriorates what users of the network think of the infrastructure. If they hold the network in low regard, they will not care for it as well as they otherwise would.

Distribution Hardware

Typically distribution hardware such as multiport hubs, switches, routers and bridges are secured behind a locked door in the server room with the server and other storage devices. Each manufacturer has their own specific commands or user interfaces for configuring these devices. This subject is treated later. The focus of this chapter is to determine if they are functional and secure. Also, their specific location should be noted on the now growing network diagram.

The diagram should show the distances from the demarcation point and the longest distances from the server room to the most remote nodes on the network. It should also clearly identify the order of the distribution hardware as you find it. Note the first piece of hardware that is connected to the cable coming from the demarcation point. It could be a packet shaper, router, switch or bridge depending on the architecture chosen. Note each subsequent piece of hardware in line including the server and any other CPUs in the server room.

It is important to point out that the assessment is not intended to be a time for repairing network bottle necks, but a tool to help discover them and suggest solutions. In spite of this, many network administrators were never formally trained in network architecture and some networks are simply hacked together and often work out of luck. I have assessed numerous networks and am amazed at the creative methods used to design them often without any consideration for efficiency or optimal performance.

Make a note in the documentation if any of the pieces of hardware are not functional. This might identify the cause of existing problems once all of the data is collected.

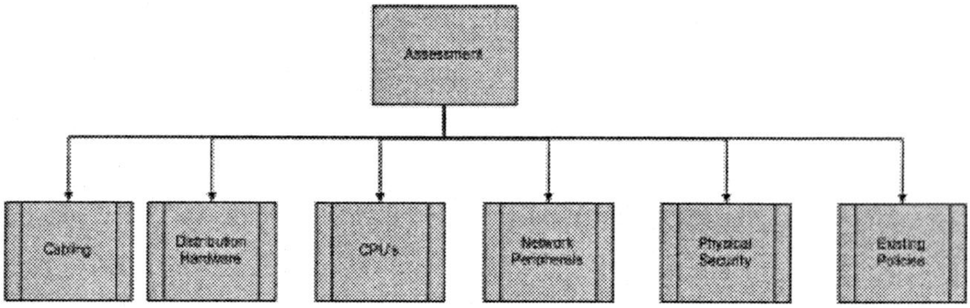

Central Processing Units (CPU's)

First, count the CPUs that should be connected to the network. This information should be included in the documentation. I recommend including the manufacturers identifier, serial numbers, MAC addresses, amount of installed memory, processor power, hard drive capacity, peripheral hardware such as CD-ROM or DVD and USB ports and any PCI cards that have been installed after purchase. This information is useful when determining capacity of a network, building rendering farms, understanding what software can and cannot be installed and also when auditing user activity on a network.

Normally a good administrator has a naming convention for the CPUs. One administrator chose cartoon character names, another a number system. The names are configured in the operating system and it is easy to identify the CPU and immediately know the capacity limitations. Knowing this serves to speed the process of trouble shooting desktops, servers and supporting CPUs.

Note in the documentation the software installed on each CPU and locate the licensing information for all installed software. During the assessment phase, the focus is to identify licensed and unlicensed software. Later, this can become an issue. If you are or become the administrator of the computer network, you will later want to bring all CPUs into compliance with the law. Downloading and using commercial software without proper licensing is illegal; it is tantamount to stealing. Well managed networks do not permit users to install their own software. This helps to keep the network in compliance.

It is important to identify if there are variations in the operating systems used and even variations in the generations of operating systems. This information is useful when trying to troubleshoot desktop issues.

Networked Peripherals

Printers, scanners, DVD burners and projectors can all be connected and managed in a network environment. Each networked item receives an IP address and possesses a MAC address. As you document the network, these nodes should also be named and located on the network diagram.

Physical Security of Server and Storage Devices

It is imperative to secure the server(s) in a locked, air controlled room that is large enough to work in without the risk of physically damaging any of the hardware or cabling. This seems so obvious. However, in two network environments I worked in, neither server room was locked. There was no air conditioning in either room and the temperature in the summer would reach 115 degrees in the room. There were multiple servers for a variety of functions and two of those servers were lost due to overheating of the mother boards.

Limiting physical access to the server room is also essential. It should not be easy to use the room as storage or as casual working space. During the assessment phase, determine who has access to the room and for what purpose. There should be adequate clearance around all of the servers and distribution hardware in the room. Determine how the hardware is secured to racks and if the racks can be locked. Document the existing conditions of the server room.

Take notice of the location of fire suppression systems, especially ceiling mounted water fire suppression systems. In the event of a fire, obviously the safety of people comes first, but it is also possible to plan for the safety of server room hardware. Make note in the documentation of how fires are suppressed and the proximity of the server room to outdoor safety. Local codes may require water based fire suppression in which case there is a very short period of time during which you can safely salvage a server. Make sure you understand how to deal with live electricity in the event the water is spraying in the server room. If you do not know how to deal with this, leave the server room and evacuate to safety.

Existing Policies

Sadly, it is very normal to discover there are no effective or comprehensive policies in place that govern users, data security, reporting of crimes and continuity. Determine if any policies have been written and properly adopted. The writing and implementation of these policies will be covered later, but during the assessment phase, document all existing (or non-existing) written policies.

Read the policies that exist. Note in the documentation any discrepancies between the written policies and what actually exists in the network. This will come in handy later.

The assessment and documentation of a network should happen prior to taking on any role as network administrator. It will help identify potential or existing problems but it will also serve as a baseline of activity that preceded your total access to the network. Preserve the documentation and copy it to the owner of the system. The politics of network administration are such that your primary working relationship is with the owner of the system or the individual she or he has designated to undertake the ownership role. Do not immediately trust the administrator unless you have been instructed to do so. Keep the assessment phase a clean and impartial process that is nothing more than a statement of fact.

Chapter 4
Developing, Writing, Implementing and Testing Security Policies

Chapter Objectives

- The need for a well planned and executed security policy
- Several questions must be answered before a policy can be formulated
- The four basic steps taken to develop a security plan:
  - ✓ Review risks and business needs of the organization
  - ✓ Be specific when addressing issues
  - ✓ Educate, Advise and Implement
  - ✓ Review and Modify regularly

Up to this point, we have discussed basic networking concepts and documented the existing network as it is. To proceed through basic computer security and then on to some advanced issues, it will be important to map the way to an end point. We need to know what we want to secure, how to secure it and how this affects the actions of legitimate users. What we need is a well planned, written security policy.

Usually, there are no security policies in place, especially in a home or small business network. I have discovered this even in large, complex enterprise environments. Security policies seem like a tedious chore until it is too late.

Policies in printed form do not necessarily prevent malicious attacks on a network; they need to be adopted and implemented and they need to properly address the security issues specific to each network. The process of developing security policies begins with a thorough reading of the assessment completed in Chapter 3. This documentation will show how the networks stands today without commentary or judgment.

An astute administrator will already have an opinion about how secure the network environment is. Now, the work of shaping a living document that will grow with the network and provide levels of security begins.

When I begin the policy phase, I have a lot of questions that I do not ask duing an assessment phase. Does the documentation reveal a carefully planned internal and external strategy for securing data and computing assets? Are there regular updates of virus protection and are the procedures for this clearly stated? Is there a clear policy regarding who can access certain files and is this properly implemented in the server operating system? Is there a clear understanding of the possible environmental hazards in the area and have proper mitigation procedures been put in place to minimize the effects of them? How does a new employee get a log in and password and how is that password managed; could I easily gain access to restricted files by lifting another employees keyboard and seeing their password? Can anyone access the wireless system? As the company adds new employees and grows, is there a plan in place that scales the network and the security at the same time? What happens if an employee or member of the family steals movies or downloads patently offensive material; are procedures in place to properly handle this issue? Is there a regular procedure for taking highly sensitive data to secure storage? Who is the keeper of the administrative password and how widely is that password distributed? Is there a concerted effort to properly plan for the dismissal or voluntary departure of key IT personnel?

At each new location where I work or consult, the answers to these questions are usually negative. Most organizations wing it until there is a problem. Without a clear policy, say, for viewing and downloading even legal pornography, attempts to fire the person who does this will probably fail. The result may be a sexual harassment lawsuit from people who are offended by the activity and the inability of the organization to stop it.

Without a complete and thoroughly tested policy, the downloading of pornographic material is a very small problem when you consider what else could happen. Further, once a policy is in place, it must be monitored for compliance and subsequently enforced. Attempting to discipline an employee with a policy that is not consistently monitored or enforced will probably fail and may result in a lawsuit being filed by the employee.

The chapters that follow might serve as a framework for a security policy, or you may choose to combine topics and even delete some that do not affect your operations. This chapter is intended to help you develop a written policy that will lead to a secure network. These then are the four basic steps toward developing an effective security policy:

Review potential risks and the business needs of the organization

Address specific issues with specific policies.

Educate, advise and then implement the policy

Review and modify the policy on a regular basis

Review potential risks and the business needs of the organization

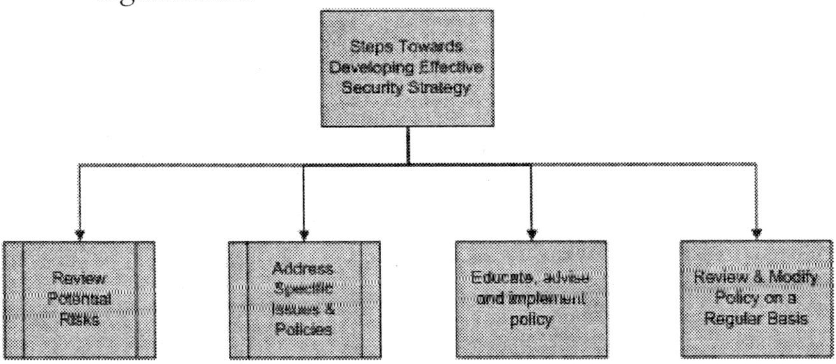

As I suggested in the first chapter, there are specific aspects of a networked environment that are at risk. I divided network assets into four main categories: Physical Security, Connectivity, Hardware and Software Infrastructure and Data.

What is essential now is to place a value on everything that falls within these categories. A database of customer names might regularly yield a company $3million in sales in any given year. Is that the face value of the database if it was destroyed or stolen? How much could you insure the database for? A new rack of blade servers in a data center with all distribution hardware intact might cost about $300,000. How quickly does this value depreciate once it is in place and what is it's value one month, one year and five years after implementation? A proprietary CRM application cost $400,000 to plan, write and implement. If someone was able to penetrate the security and ruin this application rendering it worthless, what value does that have in replacement and loss of business?

I cannot give you the numbers for these losses, yet you will need them in order to decide on a cost effective security plan. The owner of these assets needs to decide how secure to make the network based on the value of the assets being protected. It's the same principle as a physical object. The British government spends sizeable sums of money protecting the crown jewels. A neighbor we had when I was in high school spent absolutely no money protecting the pile of old tires he had in his back yard. Translating that across to a computer network, if you have a few games and your favorite internet links on your computer, security is not much of a worry. But, if you are holding the electronic versions of plans for futuristic weapons in the Department of Defense, you spend time and money on security.

I make this point because many security plans fail when a proper value assessment is not made of assets and the security is either cost prohibitive to protect valueless assets or extremely valuable assets are permanently lost because no security was implemented. Provide security commensurate with the value of the asset.

Address Specific Issues with Specific Policies

A Director of a well funded program sat red faced as local police investigated the loss of a data base of donors. The donors might have continued to give to the program, but the issue was not so much the loss of the database but the revelation of the value of personal assets belonging to the donors. Some of the information became public and an extortion attempt followed to suppress the remainder of the personal data. The Director had agreed to purchase an expensive firebox in addition to upgrading the routers. Everyone sat comfortable behind a well guarded external firewall. The data was stolen from the inside as the network administrator watched dutifully at the perimeter for intrusions.

In another case study, a company spent thousands of dollars on anti-virus and operating systems updates but failed to properly analyze the physical security of their building and fifteen computers, including the servers and the data farm, were carried effortlessly out the door. The antivirus applications might have been necessary, but they could also have been excessive. What was not considered was the potential loss from theft. Maybe an alarm system and better locks would have been a better first purchase followed later by the antivirus protection.

It is important to list all of the potential risks, and once they have been prioritized by dollar value and importance to operations, address each in a manner consistent with their value. This might show up in the security policy as procedures for very basic anti virus updating and procedures for extensive monitoring of physical security. This would make sense in a networked environment where internet access was not necessary and therefore there was little or no exposure to outside viruses, but the company is located in an area that either experiences high crime rates or the exits are obscured with landscaping.

The subsequent chapters in this book offer practical methods for securing each aspect. These methods can be the basis of that portion of the security policy and modified to respond to the hierarchy of value placed on computing assets.

Educate, Advise and then implement the policy

Once all of the risks have been evaluated and a proper response formulated, the policy is not going to be effective until people understand why it was written, what it hopes to attain, how it impacts their behavior and then becomes a mandatory part of their terms of employment. You will probably need a lawyer to get through this.

Most managers now know that if they do not have written policies that are mandatory and presented and consented to in writing by the employee, they virtually have no policies. This is really the easy part, though. After an introduction period, employees are required to sign an acceptance form of the new policies, there is a stated implementation date and following that date they must comply with the new policies. A good lawyer will make fast business of this part.

The difficulty in introducing security policies, even after they become mandatory, is to get people to follow them. I would much rather have buy-in to the policy and willing participation than to have to fire someone because they forgot to lock the server room door. This requires education.

The most troublesome security breakdown is the tendency people have to write passwords in a notebook or on a slip of paper and keep them within arms length of the keyboard in a drawer, under the keyboard or pinned to the cubicle wall. Worse yet, an employee calls in sick, calls a friend at work and gives him all of her passwords to check her email. Even when there were specific policies in place and the employee agreed to the policy in writing, I have conducted physical audits of workstations only to find eighty to ninety percent of the employees violating this policy. Even when the CEO warned them of reprimand and that the passwords would be confiscated and changed, many employees still failed to comply with the policy.

In both private commercial and academic environments, the need to provide a clean, safe and comfortable working environment is paramount and this covers the viewing and downloading material others would find immoral or out right offensive. A security policy should also cover this and the topic needs to be discussed during routine sexual harassment presentations as well as upon hire.

It is advisable to conduct comprehensive network security training during orientation. Cover all issues pertaining to employee activity and behavior that affect the network.

In the enforcement of security policies, there has to be an iron fist inside a velvet glove. Violations of the security policy affect operations and could diminish profits. Berating and humiliating someone for an accidental violation might serve to break down morale and future desire to observe policies and I have known cases where employees have turned on their companies and tried to wreck as much harm as they could on the network after being humiliated. There might be cause for immediate dismissal, but all of this from innocent slip ups of password management to outright intentional destruction of data should be handled professionally and in compliance with local human resource laws.

It's not funny to think of the number of network administrators who have nick names like Atilla the Hun and worse. Security Policies can be very powerful and might best be kept out of the hands of the power hungry. The policies are intended to secure the environment, assets and data.

Review and modify the policy on a regular basis

As conditions change, so must the security policy. This includes the introduction of new databases, new operating systems, new divisions within the company and any change necessary to accommodate growth. A company might begin to allow employees the ability to surf the net whereas they did not previously allow it. This elevates the need for constantly updating antiviral protection. An outsourced company may be retained to provide desk top back up for all workstations and this would change how employees and internal administrators would deal with desk top issues.

In one specific chapter later in this book, I will deal with scaling a network to accommodate growth but with security paramount in mind. New architectures are being introduced that help achieve secure, scalable environments and often an organization must put aside the revered DMZ and firewall and do something differently to satisfy the needs of the business. I note that here because of the number of administrators who do not educate themselves on emerging trends but instead hang on to really old school methodologies that might be relatively secure but diminish potential performance.

Testing Security Policies

How does a company test security? Do you allow someone on the outside to try and attack your systems? Do you plant someone on the inside to roam the hallways and try to gather whatever data they can and see if there are internal leaks? Yes to both.

There are legitimate companies who do "white hat" testing of external security. There are fewer companies who have staff well trained enough to test the internal systems. This is new to the industry.

External penetration testing will require written permission by the ultimate owner of the system and the specifications will be very clear as to what the test is looking for. Most legitimate penetration tests stop at the open port and proceed no further. Their report will make clear what they found and what the vulnerabilities are. This kind of test should be typically completed without the knowledge of the network administrator. Advanced knowledge of the test would possibly allow them to examine their own configurations ahead of time and make some corrections. This might be the desired outcome, but it is always good to have a silent and objective analysis of the system security.

The internal tests are a little more difficult to plan and implement, but they should include some social engineering to determine if personnel are sharing passwords, an audit of attempts to access restricted drives or files, a physical audit of workstations to see if passwords are easily accessible and an audit of workstations to determine of internet use is within compliance with company policies. I have always consulted with company attorneys before conducting this kind of internal audit. I first want to know if the employees are aware the owner of the company has declared in advance the possibility of this happening and the employee acknowledged this in writing. Without prior notice, it is always difficult to proceed with further education or disciplinary action for violations of policy.

I have always warned owners that they might not like what they see during the security audit. Their most treasured employee or the nephew they are helping out might turn out to be extremely careless in their practices or worse malicious in attempts to destroy or steal data.

A good test will reveal any possible weaknesses. More importantly, internal weaknesses might point to a need to conduct more education on the need for security and the policies that define them.

Chapter 5
Preventing Loss Due To Environmental Hazards

Chapter Objectives

- Try to prevent common environmental hazards
- Prepare workstations and server rooms for common local catastrophes
- Assess the risk potential of common hazards
- Assess the system in these areas

  ✓ From Demarcation to Server Room
  ✓ In the Server Room
  ✓ Workstations
  ✓ Infrastructure

I admit my mistakes. The only time I have ever lost hardware, software or data in my twenty years of managing computer resources was when I was writing several emails at Christmas to catch friends and family up on my life and I spilled a hot drink on my laptop keyboard. The mother board was shot and in those days there were no discount electronics stores basically giving them away. That hard drive was corrupted, and a company was glad to bid to retrieve the data. The cost of repairing the laptop and retrieving data then was prohibitively expensive and I just waved it off.

The data was stored on various media and oncc I could afford a new laptop, I was up and running.

I worked for several years in an academic environment that prided itself in offering to students almost the most current technology available, and for the most part it was very good hardware. Most students could not afford the CPUs we bought for the labs and we refreshed the labs every six months. That kind of commitment placed a higher level of importance on keeping them operating in optimum condition.

The biggest threat we experienced in our labs was not crackers or viruses; it was a bottled beverage with high levels of caffeine. This beverage is often a favorite of gamers and people who spend long hours in front of a computer and over seven years administering one specific network, I suffered the loss of mother boards, keyboard, cd rom drives and even printers because users would place bottles of this beverage on the hardware. When it was bumped, and it was inevitably bumped, it spilled; usually into a keyboard but often enough into a mother board or cd rom drive to always be a concern.

Coffee was the second biggest culprit. After that it was just food in general. In a student lab, sticky food is not a serious issue. In an office environment, where employees have regular access to the same workstation, food is always an issue. Sweet rolls, mayonnaise, birthday cake; you name it I pulled or wiped it out of CPUs, keyboards, mice, scanners, printers...you get the idea. People are careless with food and try hard to cover up their droppings, often blaming other people. This should be covered also in your security policy.

In February of 2001, the Seattle area witnessed a fairly severe earthquake which knocked down some brick buildings in the old part of the city. Among the ruins, sitting for several days out in the elements and under crushed brick, were numerous workstations, distribution hardware and servers, many of which were processing or storing extremely important data when the earthquake struck. First, even if the hard drives were in tact, owners were not allowed to retrieve them until city engineers allowed access into the buildings.

In the facility I was managing, we had secured the workstations to the legs of steel desks. We were not thinking of earthquake protection when we did this, rather I had experienced the theft of some RAM and I was motivated to slow down the thieves. I replaced the CPU cover screws and zip tied the case to the steel legs. During the earthquake, I recalled some emergency preparedness training; the best thing to do during and earthquake was to get under a steel desk which would probably support the collapse of the false ceiling and even some structural material. I instructed everyone in the lab to crawl under the desks. As we tumbled and shook, I noticed the CPUs stood secure and motionless. I suffered zero loss of hardware during the quake while a contemporary lost several workstations that fell from tops of cabinets or on to cement floors.

In the rest of this chapter, I want to focus attention on how to prevent human caused or natural disaster from affecting you computing resources. We can get ready for many disasters, but not all. There is no way to predict many of the worst natural disasters and even if we do prepare, there is no guarantee against loss of data or computing assets. This Chapter will set you in the right direction and over time you will improve on this for your own local circumstances.

The action items that follow can also be used to help prevent theft of computing assets. Theft of data will require a different consideration.

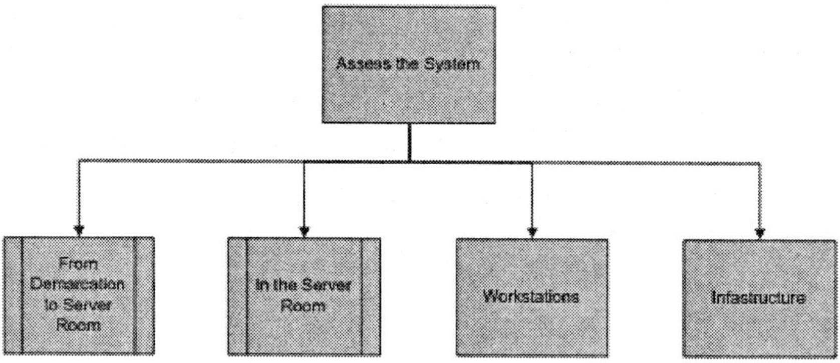

From the Demarcation Point to the Server Room

If you had the opportunity to visually trace the media that is connecting the demarcation point to the server room during your assessment, you are aware of any exposure of this cable to sharp objects, excessive heat and if the cable is susceptible to being cut by falling objects. Determine any risk to this cable and mitigate by eliminating the sharp objects and excessive heat or by re-running the cable through heat and crush resistant conduit.

A private school funded and governed by many of Seattle's elite business people suffered a complete loss of network services because the cable from the demarcation point to the server room was tacked to a ceiling and in some cases drooped down low enough a person could touch it, and they did with a pair of bolt cutters in five or six places. If you can too easily see and trace this cable, do whatever you can to conceal it.

At the Server Room

If the organization does not currently have rack mountable hardware and a server/hardware rack that is secured to the floor and wall, start planning on getting them. Loosely stacked hardware is going to fall or get kicked and there is a risk of losing the hardware or connectivity easily.

Securing hardware to a rack will increase the possibility of limiting damage in the event of a fire.

As stated previously, check for fire suppressant sprinkler heads and observe how it is possible in the event of a false alarm to safely remove the hardware and prevent water damage. I know of a handful of administrators who have successfully prevented water damage in the event the fire sprinklers were set off, but in every case the alarms were false and there was no real danger of fire. In the case of a real fire, evacuate safely and let the fire department do their job. Serves are easily replaced, people are not.

Check out the local flood tables in your area. Each county government keeps statistics on the potential of flooding and records what are known as fifty and one hundred year floods. Some developers were given permission to build on flood plains or they built in former wet lands and the seasonal rain water had not been properly mitigated. This is true in almost any part of the country as we develop more and more. I was witness to flash flooding in Eastern Colorado that wiped out an industrial park. I would watch every year as a shopping mall in Washington State would experience some level, sometimes sever, of flooding because they built over wetlands. If your business operations are on the ground level, don't assume you will never be flooded. Be certain. Racking the hardware two or three feet off the ground will help prevent damage from natural flooding as well as flooding caused by broken water pipes or a leaky roof.

Workstations

Here is where you need to make some local command decisions. Aside from energy beverages being poured the mother boards, decide on the most critical risks to labs and desk top workstations. Once I knew we were well out of the one hundred year flood plain, I chose to secure the workstations in labs to the steel desk legs. I used several plastic zip ties and it took us an average of ten minutes to completely free a workstation. I decided this was an inexpensive way to slow down and perhaps discourage the thieves. As I noted earlier, this also served as a measure of security against a major earthquake.

After I left this position, the area suffered a record setting wind storm and a large tree fell on the tilt up concrete building. The wood structure roof and the false panel ceiling were partially crushed where the tree hit and the debris landed on desk surfaces and none of the workstations were damaged. Only one monitor was damaged and quickly replaced.

I was also confident enough in the general structure of the building when we moved in to determine that the roof had been replaced as part of our improvement contract and leaks were not likely. If I had thought the roof was potentially a flooding source, I would have tried to create a local solution that attempted to consider all of these potential risks. The desired outcome of this process is a seasoned policy that covers as much as can be covered knowing there will be a constant review as the business grows.

Chapter 6

Preventing Identity Theft, Chat-Sniffing, Cyber-Stalking and Cyber-Bullying

Chapter Objectives

- Understand why people want to steal data
- Security Issues with Instant Messaging
- Analyze the following areas for exposure:
    - ✓ Membership Information
    - ✓ Instant Messaging Identity
    - ✓ Social Engineering
    - ✓ Cyber identities
- Special Issues with Cyber Bullying and Stalking

It is not an Urban Legend about the guy who responded to a seemingly personal email from the Secretary of Finance of an African country. He was lured into a scam where he needed to "finance" the transition of millions of dollars from off shore accounts to his account and he was guaranteed the millions of dollars in interest and finders fees for his generous efforts. Of course, the thirty five thousand dollars hr fronted for the "financing" end of the bargain disappeared and the while thing was a scam. There has been more than one victim of this.

Understanding why people want your personal information will help determine best methods for preventing theft. There are predators who want information about children or adults so they can stalk and abuse them. There are laws that prevent websites from even allowing children to identify themselves. Adults can identify anything they like about themselves for all to read. Also, social security numbers, birthdates, addresses, job titles and other types of personal financial information is easily used to secure credit cards, loans and any other type of financial service. At one company, a highly trusted receptionist was arrested for using this kind of information from sixteen employees to illegally acquire credit cards which he used to pay off other credit cards. Finally, given the proper amount of information, a person could use your identity to conduct illicit or illegal activity on a computer. Spoofing techniques when properly applied can even make it appear as if the perpetrator used your computer.

Instant messaging is a common internet activity that yields the best quality personal identity information for potential thieves. Users of messenger services are advised when they install and configure theses applications not to include information such as bank account and social security numbers in the messages. This information can be seen by anyone with a cheap chat sniffing software application. Many companies and organizations block and uninstall messenger services for this and other security reasons. Many user policies are explicit in not allowing the use of messenger services, especially in grade schools.

Messenger services use a protocol that exchanges information in plain text, as if you were writing a message in Notepad or some other plain text application. These patterns of ones and zeros are easily intercepted and reproduced by anyone with the sniffing software.

A security assessment of a bank in the Seattle area pin pointed the cause of huge information leaks regarding customer account information; bankers were chatting internally and externally with staff and customers putting names, addresses, account numbers, dollar figures and even social security numbers in these chat sessions. The use of instant messaging was banned immediately.

Finally, knowing who is reading your blog, chat sessions and email will help reduce the theft of personal information. Unwittingly, even children who contribute to these types of online forums include information about themselves that would allow a predator to identify and locate them. This might be perfectly acceptable, but in many cases it is not. Friendship web portals where students identify themselves in association with their school can and has lead to stalking.

The internet and the tools developed for communicating there are a double edged sword. They allow for immediate and effective communication and introductions between people who might otherwise never meet. Knowing who and where you are can lead to stealing personal information or heaping abuse on you as a victim of stalking or bullying. The action items that follow will help prevent the loss or abuse of personal information. Let's focus on action items to help prevent abuse or theft of personal data by mitigation of Membership; Information; Instant Messaging; Social Engineering; Cyber Identity.

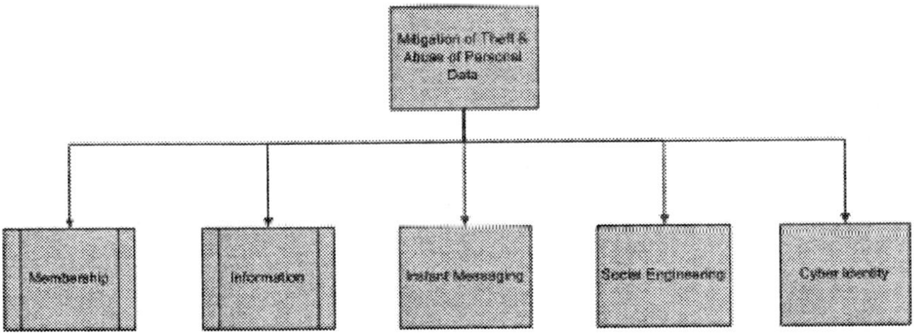

Membership Information

I am not an advocate of lying when creating user profiles for email and web portals. There is usually the option of not adding information such as a real name, address, age or anything else the portal requests. A clever moniker with no photograph or any other personal information usually allows the user to proceed and enjoy the benefits of the cyber community. If this is not an option, consider the value of membership against the potential of abuse of personal information. Most free email, dating, or social cyber communities will allow anonymous membership with the option of adding more information later by updating a profile.

The use of professional cyber communities to gain access to research materials often requires the member to clearly identify many aspects of their profession, even their salary range. The member gets free access to valuable information at the expense of completing extensive personal profiles. I have declined most of these especially when they request information about my age, salary, job title, company and level of education. In spite of promises the information is for their edification only, I am aware of the market for demographic information that is sold to spamming professionals. Many other Information Technology professionals openly admit to lying in these profiles just to get the information without giving away valuable personal and professional information.

Take the time to view the personal profile for every email address, cyber community membership and chat room you belong to. Remove or conceal any information you would not want a stranger to know.

Instant Messaging

Third party applications can be purchased to encrypt instant messaging. Most of them require both parties to have the same application. This is a strategy deployed by some companies; instant messaging would then be allowed within the confines of the company since no outsider would have legitimate access to the corporate licensing and would therefore not have the software and configurations needed to decrypt the messages.

If encrypting messages is not a practical solution, continue using instant messaging as if you are having a conversation with someone in a room full of strangers who can hear and copy every word. This same principle applies to chat rooms, discussion forums and any other type of real time exchange of cyber information. It is also important to remember when using chat rooms. Certain kinds of information exchange can be considered criminal activity, such as making threats on the life of another person. Every word contributed to the chat room is preserved. It might be difficult but rarely impossible to identify the person contributing illegal content to a chat session.

Social Engineering

When someone overhears a conversation in a coffee shop and jots down personal identifiers, this is not yet illegal. What they do with the information might be. This is a very pernicious form of social engineering. There was an expression during world war two that was used to caution people not to talk about where their loved ones were located; Loose Lips Sink Ships. Keep this in mind when discussing passwords, account information and anything else that someone could use.

When I was an administrator in a private school, one of the instructors had the ability to watch my hands as I typed a very complex password to gain administrative access. I was not aware he was watching and later caught him managing a workstation after entering the password. I now always ask people to turn away as I type in any password. Many administrators, myself among them, become suspicious of anyone acting too kindly and asking for information about the network they otherwise should not have. I simply smile and tell them not to take it personally; when it comes to data security I trust no one.

During routine internal audits in a major corporation, the auditor would ask for keys that would give him unrestricted access to all staff level workstations. In spite of numerous warnings, the auditor would inevitably find log in names and passwords written on scraps of paper and either hidden under the keyboard or pinned to a bulletin board by the workstation. Imagine the fun one could have with someone else's access. Educate personnel on the risks of poor password management; anyone with after hour access to the workstation can log on as that person and gain access to personal or company data or conduct illicit and illegal activity on the internet under the name of the person who left their password lying around.

Assessing Cyber Identities

Try a few common methods used to capture personal information from the internet. Launch your web browser and use whatever search engine you prefer. Google is good, but there are other engines that will produce different results. In the search engine, type your full name. My search usually results in about twenty links that contain information about my books, my employer, my work as a board member for a charitable organization, a link to a short story I wrote. People I lost track of over the years used this method to find me. They were able to ascertain my employer, get my email address and even discovered through news articles about my books where I would appear for a book singing. One person, whom I like and respect, showed up at the signing in order to renew a long lost friendship.

Fortunately, when I search my own name I do not find any derogatory information. When assisting others, however, this is not the case. People of every age are vulnerable to negative, libelous statements that someone might post in a cyber community or on a website.

Cyber bullies target teenage peers using this tactic, creating horrific lies about the victim and letting anyone who cares read the forum, chat room or blog postings. These postings are frequently available through search engines. It is common now for teenagers to advertise what they have posted about their victims and encourage other peers to access the sites and read the damaging information or view an embarrassing photograph.

If you find false and negative information on a website, contact the webmaster immediately. There is a contact link for every webmaster. If you find false and negative information on a social cyber-community, contact the manager for that site immediately. In both cases, demand the information be removed. By law, they must remove the negative information until the poster can prove the information is of public record, such as a criminal or civil judgment.

If you are a victim of cyber bullying or if an adult tries to have a conversation about sexual activity with children you know or you experience any other kind of exchange of information that could be considered illegal, report the activity immediately to your local police authorities. Do not respond to the abuser unless specifically instructed to do so by the police.

It is worth noting in this chapter the concept of proper preservation of evidence. Take a course sometime from a community college offering degrees in criminal justice on cyber-evidence or invite local law enforcement to speak to a group about preserving evidence. It will help you help the police capture and convict those who choose to steal your identity or to conduct illegal activity on the internet. Do not ever try to police the internet yourself; you will only help the perpetrators.

Chapter 7

Securing Wireless Networks

Chapter Objectives

- Wireless networks use radio frequencies, and these are not secure
- There is no law against monitoring data over wireless
- Understand the difference between WEP and WPA
- Methods of securing a wireless network:

  ✓ Enable WEP or WPA
  ✓ Disable DHCP
  ✓ Stop Broadcasting SSID
  ✓ Use MAC filtering
  ✓ Use Complex Passwords
  ✓ Reduce the Effective Range

Wireless networking has experienced huge growth in the last several years. Anyone with a basic network connection whether through dial up, adsl, dsl, cable or satellite can inexpensively network desktops and laptops at home or in a small office environment. Most laptops have built-in wireless networking interface cards and for about twenty dollars a wireless networking interface card can be installed in either a desktop or laptop.

Wireless networking depends on equipment that is slightly different from standard hard wired networking. The internet connection enters at the same demarcation point and is distributed then through a cable modem to typically a router that distributes the Internet Protocol addresses to the computers on the network. Instead of then being distributed through hard wire, another device, the Wireless Access Point, distributes the data over the network via radio waves.

Radio waves are nothing more than the distribution of low voltage electricity from a transmitter to a receiver. It's the same principle as the little am radio I used to listen to the Seattle Pilots baseball team in the wood shed. That is before they left Seattle and went to become the Milwaukee Brewers. Yes, I have let go and forgiven them.

The range of these radio waves depends on what is known as the Hertz range, or the frequency of the radio waves. Wifi is now distributed at 2.4 gigahertz and has an effective "clear shot' range of 300 feet. The effective distribution range diminishes for every wall, ceiling or roof the frequency must travel through. Generally, each solid obstruction reduces the effective range by about 50-100 feet.

Whenever I need immediate internet access to check email, I boot my laptop and search for wireless networks within an effective range. In Seattle, I often detect twenty to thirty networks in some neighborhoods. I look for public wireless networks that are configured to allow anyone with a proper network interface card to connect to the network and access the internet.

Some businesses and schools set up wireless access for customers and students and an administrator must create an access account which can be free or the business can charge a fee for access. These networks are slightly more secure than those networks I find that have no restrictions and are owned by individuals or small businesses.

There is yet no law that prohibits connecting to a wireless network that has not been secured to restrict access to specific individuals. It is against the law to gain any illicit access to any computer or other kind of node connected to this wireless network. This creates a security dilemma. Unsecured wireless networks use the public airwaves at 2.4 gigahertz and any laptop or hand held device that has the capability to receive and transmit over this network can.

To illustrate again the risks here, there are very inexpensive chat sniffing applications that allow anyone to capture and read in real time most chat messages that are sent over a wireless network. A computer does not necessarily need to be connected to the network to capture the messages, but using an unsecured access to a wireless network allows the computer user to determine the IP addressing configuration for the network and this makes the chat sniffing even easier. Again, if the chat messages are not encrypted and they are transmitted over a wireless network, these are in the public domain. If a person uses the information subsequently for some illicit or illegal activity, then they have broken the law.

It is easy to understand why a wireless network is not secure. It might be that a wireless network is not important enough to be a target or there is no one in the neighborhood or business-park who even cares to access the network, but this is simply not enough assurance. Data transmitted and stored on a wireless network is extremely vulnerable.

One method that has been commonly used to secure access to the network is encrypting an access control password using Wired Equivalency Protection (WEP) and Wi-Fi Protected Access (WPA). How to use these will be explained a bit later in this chapter, but my concern here is how these encryption methods are touted. One security specialist explained to several elderly participants in a lecture that once WEP or WPA are enabled, all data crossing over the network is then encrypted. This is not the case at all. Other applications must be used to encrypt specific data; WEP and WPA encrypt access permissions and they restrict access to the network. It is also well known among crackers that WEP can be "cracked" in a matter of minutes and the hacker can gain easy access to network services. Obviously, they have broken the law as it is illegal to access a computer network that has been specifically restricted to certain users. If you do not have the specific key to enable your computer to send and receive encrypted data for this network, you have not been given permission to use the network.

Let's look at several methods for securing a wireless network. Again, there is no guarantee that once these practices have been put into place someone will not gain access to your network. Later in the book we discuss methods of monitoring the network to determine if there have been access attempts made on the network.

We begin to secure the Wireless Network with the following:

Enabling WEP or WPA

Disabling DHCP on the wireless system

Stop Broadcasting the SSID of the Wireless Network

Use MAC address filtering

Use complex administrative passwords

Reduce the effective range of distribution

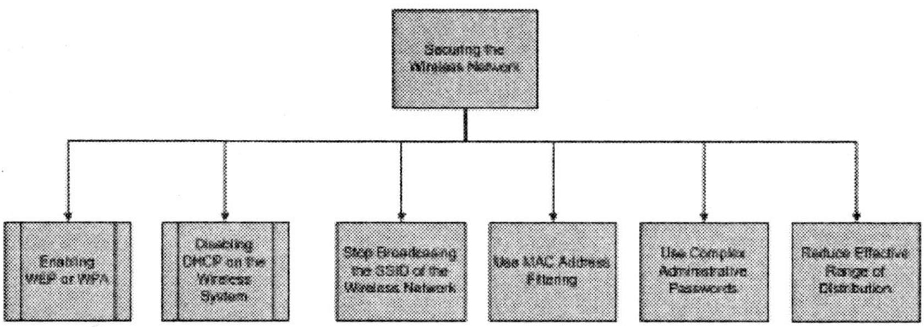

Enabling WEP or WPA

Most wireless access points now require some configuration. I have set up several different types and found the instructions easy to understand. During configuration, among other things we will cover further down, the user is asked to implement WEP or WPA. Put simply, WPA is a more rigorous encryption and should be chosen. This will slow down virtually all but a few hackers who would be very desperate to sit in your driveway running a password cracking application for an hour or more trying to gain access. An encryption key is generated by the installation software. Write this down. This is the key that must be entered into the wireless administration application in the computer. This application comes with the wireless network interface card and is used to manage all wireless network connections. To gain access to the wireless network after WPA has been installed, a dialog box will appear as the user attempts to access the network. Here is where the trusted user enters the encryption key. Obviously in a commercial environment, it would be wise to give this key only to the entrusted administrator and allow them to enter the key as each new user must gain access. Once the key has been entered the user is considered trusted and will be allowed access until the key is changed. In our chapter on policy, I will cover briefly the need to regularly change encrypted access control keys especially when a disgruntled employee leaves.

Disabling DHCP on the Wireless system

There is a protocol used to hand out IP addresses to computers on a network. This exists in the router, and could exist in a switch or a server. Once a computer is configured and authenticated, the IP address is given to the Network Interface Card and the computer can access networking services.

There is a difference between a public IP address and a private IP address sequence. Public IP addresses can be seen by other computers on different networks. Private addresses are not seen externally and cannot really access the internet unless they are routed through one public address. Most wireless devices that distribute IP addresses use one external public address and give all connected computers a private address, and these addresses are within a specific range. If a computer can see data transmitting over a wireless network, it can detect the addressing. This allows a hacker to sniff a specific range of computers using these addresses and this makes it easier to capture chat messages, email and other types of data being transmitted.

If the administrator turns off the DHCP for IP addressing, then they will enter a static address in the network interface card and this static address will be configured in the router to allow the trusted computer to access networking services. Static addresses do not need to follow any pattern and can be any combination of private addresses. This practice does not allow a chat sniffing or other type of detection application to determine any address of any computer on the network.

Stop broadcasting the network SSID

Most configurable wireless access points or routers allow for the choice to broadcast or to not broadcast the SSID. If someone parks outside your business and searches for wireless networks, if you are broadcasting the name of your wireless network, it will appear in the list of available networks on their computer. If you choose not to broadcast, the person searching for wireless networks will not see your wireless system and will not attempt to connect. However, it is very important for the administrator to remember accurately what the SSID for the system is. It is advisable to change the default SSID to some complex name and then to retain that name in a secure environment along with the WPA. When a new user is connected to the wireless, the administrator will need to enter the SSID and the encrypted key both. Again, this SSID can be changed at will but then all computers must have the new name entered before they can gain access.

Enable MAC address filtering

To gain access to a network, a computer needs a network interface card with a unique MAC address. This address is complex enough so that no two computers will have the same MAC address. The address will migrate to another computer if the network interface card is removed and installed in another computer. Some of the more complex configurable wireless access points or wireless routers provide the opportunity to list the trusted MAC addresses. Even if someone sees your wireless network, if their MAC address is not listed, they have no way of accessing any services or information on the wireless network. The administrator must find the MAC address on each computer and enter it into the list. Once a person is no longer allowed access, their MAC address can be quickly removed. Finding the MAC address is easy. In a Windows environment, the administrator runs the Command prompt, enters 'ipconfig /all' at the prompt and immediately the computer lists the IP and MAC address of the computer. The MAC address is often listed as the Machine address of the computer.

Using complex administrative passwords

As a test, students of computing science are often told to test the administrative password patterns of a given system. They are told to enter the user name Administrator in the user name field, and then they enter two different passwords. The first is 'Password', and if they have not gained access to the system, they enter the password 'God". In recent years, these two password would have granted access to almost eight percent of all managed networks. Fortunately, the word is out; create complex alpha-numeric passwords and memorize them.

Password cracking software applications are easily obtained, and the more complex the password, the more difficult they are to crack. A good practice is to create a password that is at least 16 characters long containing small letters, capitalized letters, numbers and keyboard symbols. It is also wise to maintain these passwords in the same secure environment as the WPA and SSID.

Reduce the effective range of the wireless network

The limitations of the range of effective wireless computer can work to the advantage of small home or business networks. Knowing that every wall, floor, ceiling or roof will reduce the effective range, position the wireless access points where legitimate users will gain access but outsiders will not even see a signal. Most wireless access points and routers will allow the owner to reduce the output and thereby effectively reducing the range. A good test of this is to take a wireless device outside of the premises and continue to adjust the location or output until it cannot be detected by anyone but authorized users.

While these practices will never guarantee the security of a wireless network, when combined and used together they help to increase the probability that potential illicit users will not even see the network let alone be able to gain access.

Chapter 8

Protecting from Viruses and other types of Malware

Chapter Objectives

- Understand how viruses, spy bots and rootkits are created
- Understand the difference between viruses, spy bots and rootkits
- Understand how each is introduced to the system
- These threats are not purely external, there are internal threats as well
- The importance of updating patches and regular scans

Conventional computer wisdom for so many years warned strictly against viruses attached to emails and there was relatively little emphasis placed on more pernicious forms of attacks on personal and company owned data and assets.

When I taught programming, I wanted the students to understand that a program can be written to do just about anything we want. In an introductory class, I posed a question and a project for extra credit; could the student write a program that would search for personal data in a standard Windows directory structure. Of course they succeeded, some more than others. In a more advanced programming class, these same students were offered another extra credit project. Could they write a program that could piggy back in an email attachment undetected and locate itself in a file or directory where it could monitor and log all internet activity on a given computer and further occasionally send this log file to a specific port on another computer. This is more difficult than the first, but three students were amazingly successful.

While this might be perceived as intrusive behavior, there are legitimate applications for such a program. A parent might want a legitimately licensed program that would report all internet activity on all computers at home on a regular basis. As a network administrator, I used similar log files regularly to monitor employee internet access.

In the wrong hands, however, this type of program known as a spybot is regularly a by product of a visit to websites that may or may not be related to the website content. Someone associated with the site sends the program to an open port and it functions as a monitor for illicit purposes. The spybot is not necessarily programmed to destroy data or diminish hardware functionality; its primary function is to collect specific types of data.

The viruses of the late nineties were brute force attacks on data and infrastructure. Downloading patches and antivirus updates did a fairly good job of offering protection from this type of malicious attack. However, with the rise in identify theft, corporate spying and data mining, the plan of attack has changed dramatically. Instead of destroying the data, it was more valuable to steal the data over long periods of time.

Early on, cookies placed on a computer were seen as necessary to speed up the return to any given web site, especially a site where the users has decided to allow the site to remember their log in and password. Many virtual communities and information based sites want to personalize your experience of their site so they ask you to create a membership profile. In order to reduce the number of passwords you need to memorize, these sites offer to place a cookie on your computer that holds your log in and password. When you launch the site, a program running on the site searches for the cookie and reads the log in and password and places them in the proper dialogue box. In a few seconds you are logged in.

Imagine the power of such a program in the wrong hands. A very good programmer can use this same framework for a program that is not voluntarily downloaded and that reads every keystroke on your computer and logs them in plain text. Don't stop there. Why not a program that would identify banking, tax, legal and investment accounts and copy this material to a log that is accessible to someone at a website you visit regularly.

Quietly, banks, schools and government agencies are dealing with this issue. The primary source of this type of attack is not necessarily external, and in fact the majority of these come from inside the network. One financial aid administrator for a private school hired an individual with extensive experience with federal financial aid programs. The person was really on a secret payroll of a competing school and was allowed to hire out to work the temp job offered. During his tenure, he placed five or more spybots on other financial aid workstations and the competing school was able to track certain types of data transactions which told them real numbers for enrollment, percentage of self pay versus financial aid students and other useful data. Fortunately the network administrator conducted regular audits of installed applications and discovered the programs.

Many users have become aware of these issues but have not completely strategized how to protect their networking environments. The beginning is easy; get an industry tested anti virus software for the network and individual workstations. Schedule the updates of these applications as frequently as the manufacturer allows.

The next step is to find and install security applications that specifically focus on spybots, cookies, malware and other types of data mining applications that do not fall into the category of a virus.

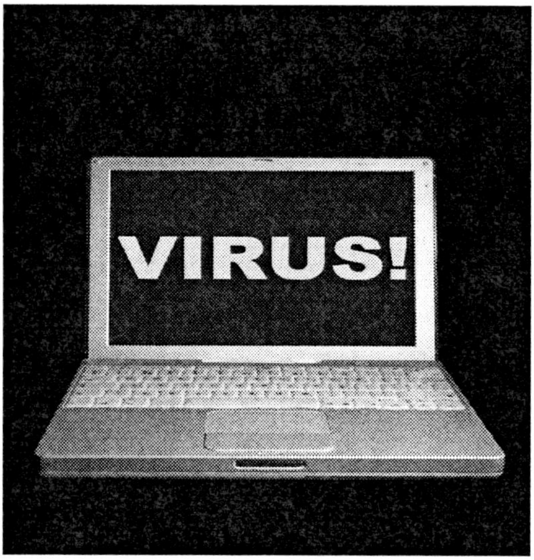

I have used Spybot Search and Destroy. It is effective at regularly scanning my hard drive for these types of applications. I also recommend doing some research on various web browsers. If you use Explorer as your default browser, go to the Microsoft website and search for information and downloads for securing Explorer. There have been known vulnerabilities and Microsoft works diligently to patch them. I recommend doing some research into Mozilla Firefox as a web browser and the companion Stopzilla which can be configured to monitor in real time for cookies, spybots and other types of malware. These products have proven to be fairly successful in keeping abreast with new versions of these problematic applications.

If you are managing a networked environment and choose to pay for automatic updating of antivirus protection and applications that clean spybots and cookies, prepare other users in advance to make sure their computers are able to receive the updates properly. In the chapter on policies, I will cover some ideas on how to effectively work with one to five thousand employees and succeed in thoroughly updating this protection.

Rootkits present a unique security challenge. These are applications used to identify at the root level what applications and processes are running on an individual workstation or on the server. As a tool for corporate spying, this data is valuable. If I own a software company selling server operating systems, I would like to know what operating system is running on any given server. With a rootkit I can see if it is my product and then check to see if it is a licensed version. I can also determine if there is a stateful chat session and determine if any data is being transmitted in that session; if not I can send a virus. The rootkit sits quietly telling the person who placed it there about applications and processes; it is the illicit use of this data that allows a cracker then to exploit the system. There are separate applications that deal directly with rootkits.

Continuously updating virus, spybot and rootkit applications is a very necessary part of a security plan. More importantly is the practice of updating all available security patches offered by the manufacturer of the operating systems in use. This can be done over the network from a centrally managed server. It will be essential, however, for users to cooperate and leave CPUs running as necessary.

Chapter 9

Understanding Hacking and Cracking

Chapter Objectives

- Hackers are known for building up and inventing
- Crackers are the truly destructive individuals
- ✓ Conditions where cracking is most apt to happen:
  - ✓ Open ports
  - ✓ Mismanaged administrative access
  - ✓ After Social Engineering
- Determine what systems are more likely to be cracked
- Understand that both the perimeter and the internal systems must be hardened

True hackers want their good reputation back. It was high-jacked by people who should properly be called crackers. The crackers are the folks who break into or simply break computer systems and destroy data. Hackers have long prided themselves on being creators and problem solvers. The true hacking community does not advocate breaking into, stealing, breaking, disrupting or in any way illicitly or illegally gaining access to systems. They advocate real problem solving in order to make computing easier and more effective.

Crackers, on the other hand, want exactly the opposite. They advocate grossly illegal activity and it is directed at computer systems. They call themselves hackers, but they are not that good, really, at what they do; they do not deserve the title. I said that to a class of programmers and immediately was threatened by two crackers who set out to destroy my computer and my data. They did not succeed. Whereas one of the very skilled programmers in the class would have easily succeeded actually was inspired to do some social engineering of the efforts of the crackers and we were able to stay a few steps ahead of them and finally thwarted their attempts.

A cracker with a high level of programming and networking skills can do damage, no doubt. There are several well publicized and as many secret case studies of data destruction, data theft, infrastructure damage and planted viruses that required some of the highest skill sets in the IT world. All of them were perpetrated by someone intent on committing a crime, even though they may have never been caught.

A system is vulnerable to these kinds of focused attacks if the following conditions are present.

First, open ports are not just an invitation to crack, but a widely broadcasted invitation. Crackers routinely scan ports of their targets and can then access the target computer quite easily if the ports are open. Going back to our discussion on Instant Messaging, the protocol that is the underlying engine for Instant Messaging, H.323, runs in what is known as promiscuous mode. The port it uses to communicate with other computers is always open and receptive especially if the "chat" is idle. The protocol is designed to allow almost any kind of file to pass into the computer through the open port. Users at the application level see that they need to give permission to download pictures or word documents through instant messaging, but in reality the protocol allows any file to enter that port.

Second, crackers search for administrative access that has not been locked down. This is a cracker's delight; an administrative account left logged in or a password that is simplistic and easy to guess. If the cracker can access a server, they are as good as in if the administrator is not constantly monitoring for intrusions. Once they have administrative access to any server on a system, they are in. One simple principle to understand is that permissions migrate; that is an administrator on one server is administrator on any other system connected to that server.

Third, crackers are great social engineers. In spite of the profile of crackers offered up to us as pimple faced teenaged males sitting in darkened basements with zero social skills, the exact opposite is true. Crackers need your passwords. They need for you to feel that you could trust them with your children, let alone your password. The crackers I have caught are intelligent, good looking, affable, party going males and females who gain your confidence and then attack. Giving them privileged access to an office or an area with several work stations and even a server room is the beginning of the end.

I never trust anyone who is too kind to me. Usually, people do not buy me drinks or dinner. When I meet a very bright and charming information technologist who is all too willing to do favors and buy refreshment, I am immediately but privately suspicious. This was an innate suspicion early on in my IT career and served me well in identifying and isolating two crackers before they could attack.

Finally, as noted previously in this book, crackers are adept at getting work where they need to steal or wreck havoc. One young man was hired because he was smooth, charming, tall, handsome and technically very bright. He had everything the owner of the financial advising company was looking for in a career IT executive. The motivations of the new hire, however, were quite different. He knew the value of the client list. He succeeded in befriending a vice president who was becoming very frustrated with the management and together they gained access to the entire client database and copied it. The FBI is pressing forward with their investigation.

Let's dispel some more of the myths about hacking and cracking. If your home computer has valuable data that is not secured, like access to your millions of dollars in various accounts, you could well be cracked. If you play games and use the internet, you probably will not be cracked. If your company has any data that might be of value to someone, you will witness an attempt, successful or not, to crack that system. If your company takes effective and easily applied measures to harden the external perimeter, the cracker will probably not succeed until they are inside your company network.

Hardening the Permieter

Later in this book we will deal specifically with perimeter and zone security. For now, of interest to the home or small business network is the need to take care of two important but easily managed tasks.

First, if you can manage your router, block all but the most essential ports. Port 80 is your internet access and if that is all you do, then block everything else. If you need to use instant messaging, find out which port this runs on and leave it open, but remember to manage your instant messaging by encrypting messages and turning the application off when a chat is finished. If you do not have a manageable router, and if you are using a Windows operating system, go to the Microsoft website and research methods for closing ports for the particular operating system you are running.

Second, check with the manufacturer of your operating system (probably Microsoft) and see if there is a resident firewall. If there is, research how to configure the resident firewall in the operating system to allow acceptable activity and to disallow external access. Do the research first. Many people have called me as an administrator wanting to know why the firewall now disallows VPN, internet access and file sharing. The answer is simple; they did not configure the firewall correctly. It would be easy to write a cookie recipe for configuring a firewall, but it may not be the configuration you need.

Once you know how to close ports and to use a resident firewall application, you have begun to secure the system from most crackers. Now you need to deal with your bigger problem; crackers inside the house.

Internal Safeguards

Much of the problem inside a networked environment is not necessarily the work of people intent on destroying data or bringing down the system. Some people are simply bored and they see the X or Z drives, click on them to see what they can access. If an administrator has not set proper permissions, they gain access to financial data and compromise the secrets of the impending public offering of stock. They doodle around a bit and accidentally delete the content of a folder. Such is the existence of the accidental cracker.

Far more sinister is the person who understands directory structures and finds a back door to sensitive information while working the help desk. With a bit of social engineering (finding someone's log in and password information within arms reach of a workstation), the perpetrator logs in after volunteering to work the late shift when no one else is around, and the deed is done and they go undetected.

It is not difficult to cause a security problem by creating a managed environment that demoralizes or humiliates employees. We laughed at a movie depicting a highly dysfunctional company that capriciously fired or promoted people without any rational grounds, and further employed supervisors who had an insatiable desire to humiliate people. The end result was an attack on their network. This has always been a concern for any network administrator. If it is not covered in the written security policy, there is usually an unwritten policy about firing someone; first disconnect their network access and delete their accounts and then fire them.

Demoralized employees represent a huge internal security risk, especially if they have not been earmarked for dismissal but they continue to hate their working environment. With little more than a motivation to "get them", a fairly bright individual can become a cracker in very little time.

Consistently I have pointed to inside perpetration of cracking as the primary concern of any security program. Any network administrator who believes the biggest problem is outside the network perimeter is inviting disaster.

Level II

Advanced Issues in Network Security

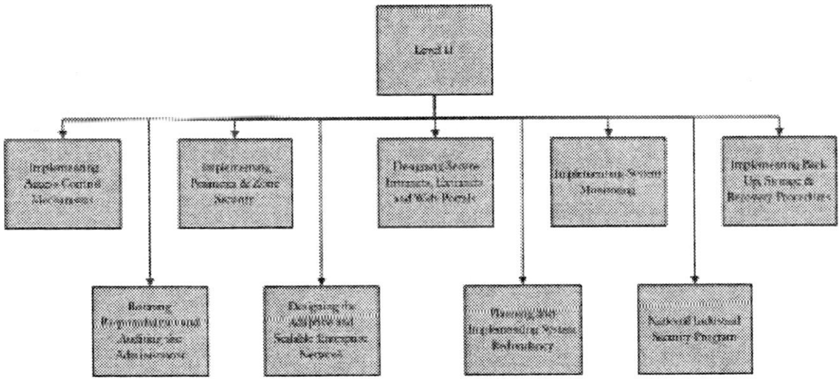

Chapter 10

Implementing Access Controls

Chapter Objectives

- Understand the need for controlling access to a network
- Two types of access vulnerabilities:
    - ✓ Unauthorized users
    - ✓ Unauthorized nodes or elements
- Unauthorized access can be inadvertent
- Unauthorized elements poses unique threats
    - ✓ Network analyzing tools can be run and capture sensitive data
    - ✓ Password cracking software can be run internally
- Access control consists of the following practices
    - ✓ Password management
    - ✓ Educating Users
    - ✓ Bio-metrics
    - ✓ Detecting all elements or nodes
    - ✓ All access to a network

The concept of Access Control is relatively easy to understand until you start to listen to the vendors of hardware and software solutions. This chapter will focus on the theory of access control and try to remain vendor free. My belief is you will be in a better position to analyze your access control mechanisms and policies if you begin with the theory and then approach vendors from that perspective.

There are two general types of vulnerabilities regarding access to a network. The first is unauthorized users and the second is unauthorized nodes or elements.

Unauthorized Users

In any given business environment, if a person is an employee or a certain category of contractor, they are given permission to use computing resources. The permission should be commensurate with the level of authority and responsibility they have in the company. This is usually accomplished with a hierarchy of permissions that determine what level of access any given individual should have.

Remote access to a computer network offers some unique challenges. While the user may have certain access rights and permissions, the method of transferring the data or accessing the network remotely may inadvertently grant access to the wrong individual. This can happen if a virtual private network (vpn) is used and is improperly configured. It can also happen if administrators do not clearly think through the issue of inheritance of permissions. As noted earlier, permissions migrate across a network backbone. If a person is granted administrative privileges on one server, other servers on the same backbone would see this person as an administrator even if he is using his own log in account. There are several lock-down solutions administrators can apply that slow down computing services and take away privileges people think they ought to have.

Guest accounts on systems have proven to be problematic for network administrators and when I am responsible for any given network, I strongly advocate against the use of them. Guests are anonymous. If the network has unrestricted access to the internet, they can at will explore and download whatever they like and the responsibility of that download falls on the administrator and owner of the computing system. A "guest" may be a very capable cracker who has the ability to challenge authentication systems and hope to crack an administrative password. Finally, an open guest account is an invitation to otherwise authorized users to bypass policies and perform illicit activities under an anonymous user name. Unless the administrator has irrefutable evidence one individual was using a specific work station when the illicit activity occurred, there is no way to prove this activity.

I have read some security policies that clearly acknowledge that an employee may need to give their log in and password to a peer, and if their respective managers approve, the access is legitimate. I disagree completely with this policy. Administrators have the highest level of access and can easily accomplish any task on any workstation and there is never a need to share access. This is a policy that will end in disaster at some point.

Later in this chapter I will discuss different strategies for creating secure access control mechanisms for users.

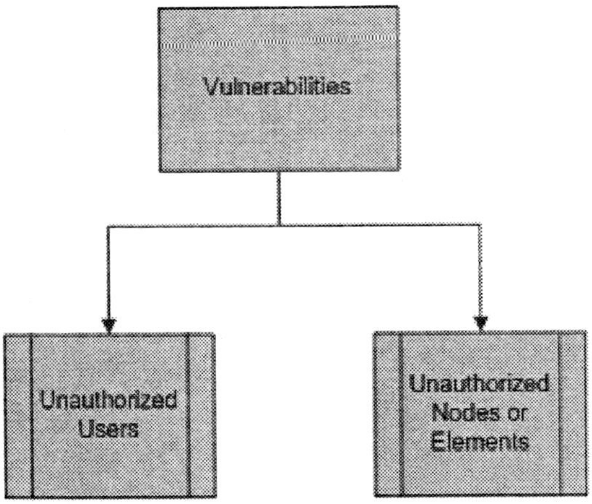

Unauthorized Nodes or Elements

Three competing electronic device manufacturers have each developed unique network analyzers. These analyzers are equipped with powerful software applications that are intended to give legitimate users valuable information about every node on a wide area network. Once plugged into an RJ45 wall jack, the user does not need authentication to see and analyze in depth every node on the system. There are software applications that can easily conduct the same level of analysis. The data received back to the device can include all IP addresses and subnets, names of computers or other nodes, operating systems running, file structures used on each node, MAC addresses, user names and many times passwords if the pass words are not hidden. These devices and applications are intended for legitimate security analyses and to map out potential bottlenecks in a network. And, even though they are costly to acquire, imagine how these devices can be abused.

Further, in a scenario where an individual left an organization in a hostile mood, it is a fairly simple procedure to note the IP addressing sequence, subnetting, device naming policies and to know the authentication process. A personally owned laptop could easily be masked to appear as if it is a company owned asset. The laptop could be equipped with password cracking software for operating systems or wireless networks. It could also just be on the network utilizing resources illicitly. If the device is granted an IP address, the user may not be able to authenticate to the system, but the node can monitor data traffic on the system, such as in the use of a chat sniff on a wireless network.

Authenticating nodes or elements on a network is equally as important as users but perhaps more difficult. Let's deal with the users first.

Access Control Mechanisms

Anyone using a network now understands the basic principle of accessing computing resources. First, they should have a user name and that is associated in a secure database with a private, complex password. The two elements, secure database and private, a complex password, are just the very foundation of an effective access control policy, but they are the most violated as well.

User name conventions are not an issue. People can try to pretend to be a user by assuming the convention, but if their name does not exist in the database, there is really no chance of them acquiring access. The real issue is in the security of the database. If it is searchable, it is going to be compromised. In Unix/Linux, the default location is /bin and any good administrator changes the location and the path immediately. In Windows, there are various methods for stand alone workstations where the owner of the computer can hide their own password. The Microsoft site will give detailed technical information about hiding password files so they are still available for authentication. While this is an essential step in providing secure access control, it is not the most troublesome.

Password management is an issue for every network administrator. A password should have at least three of four possible elements; 1) Capitalized letters, 2) small case letters, 3) numbers, 4) Keyboard characters with some exceptions. The password should be at least 12 characters in length and the sequence of the characters should be as random as possible and still allow the user to memorize it. Why? Do the math. Password crack software is based on math algorithms that query each character of the password with the question are you a letter a-z, are you a capitalized letter A-Z, are you a number 1-9 or are you a keyboard character. The cracking software then looks for patterns, something like the game on television where you start with one letter, than another and fairly soon a bright person can accurately guess the word. If the pattern appears quickly, the software begins to guess and bingo, they're in. A fast computer can ask this question of each element in the password fairly quickly, so the more characters you use, and the more random the sequence the more difficult it is to guess the password.

But this assumes someone needs to use cracking software. The worst abuse of passwords is sheer laziness.

People write the password down and place it under a keyboard or in a drawer. I have heard repeatedly the claim that they are always in their office and it is locked when they leave. So I ask these people if they know the cleaning person intimately. This is where I get the blank stare. Pretty quickly they get where I am going, but then deny anything would ever happen, in spite of the fact that it has. Some of the most notorious system cracks occurred when someone was planted on a cleaning crew and given specific instructions to find passwords. Good password management requires memorization or very secure lock-up.

I have referred to social engineering throughout this book and it remains one of the most serious security concerns for any network administrator. During mandatory Sarbanes Oxley audits, users are asked if they ever share passwords with other users. You can lie but that doesn't work for long because the person you shared the password with might not want to lie and they point to you. This is not a good position to be in. Just don't share passwords, even if you want that Friday night date and sharing a password is a prerequisite.

An alternative to passwords is bio-metrics, or the use of eye scanners and finger prints. Many people object to the use of these devices and while they are very accurate in authenticating individuals, it might become an issue in recruiting employees. I know that to be the case for at least three employers who either dismantled their bio-metric authentication or chose to stay with a password based authentication system. Alternatively, some have experimented with pass-cards, which of course can be stolen and used until the perpetrator is caught, or combined with passwords adding a layer to the authentication process.

On any given day, I might suggest rogue elements or unauthorized nodes are a more serious threat to security than compromised passwords. A network should be able to detect new elements, determine if the element is allowed access, allow or deny access based on clearly defined policies, quarantine rogue elements, locate exactly where the element is and read the MAC address that is requesting an IP address. There are numerous methods and third party products available for accomplishing this, but this type of system should be in place. If it is not, find a method or vendor and implement this.

Finally, earlier in this book I asked the reader to conduct a system assessment which included physically following the cables from the point of demarcation to the server room, and then if possible to each distribution panel and even to the wall jack. After having a new DSL system installed in one location, I diligently examined the cabling and found what is known as a vampire tap on the cable from demarcation to the server room. The device is used to monitor and capture data passing across the system. Unless a law enforcement agency has valid permission to do this, it is illegal. We were never able to determine who had placed the device and the matter was turned over to the police.

Access control is more than logging in to a system. Access control systems should control any type of access to your network. After completing the system assessment, an administrator should be able to pull information from various areas of the assessment and determine if there are adequate access controls. The assessment will point out two areas of concern; the perimeter and any internal zones of the network. Let's look at that these in the next chapter.

Chapter 11

Implementing Perimeter and Zone Security

Chapter Objectives

- Understand the concept of perimeter security
- Understand the concept of a zone architecture within a perimeter
- Good zone architecture controls access between zones.
- Perimeters are extended through VPNs and other remote access technologies
- Slack management almost guarantees bad perimeter and zone security

This concept is easy to understand if we look at a computer network as if it were a baseball stadium. I like the San Diego Padres PETCO Field for this comparison. If I want to boo the Red Sox, I buy a ticket in the cheap seats. There are a couple of good restaurants I like there and before I give my ticket over to the taker, I buy something and take it to go.

The sidewalk around the perimeter of PETCO Field reveals there is a grassy area where people can watch the game for free. The view isn't great, but they can see the game live and they haven't paid one cent. I usually buy tickets in the third tier above first base. My ticket is a specific color with a specific section and seat number on it. I give my ticket to the taker, they examine my take out food bag for weapons and booze, and I am in. I walk around the internal walkways in the stadium until I find the correct section, and then my specific seat. By now the Red Sox are on the field and I can boo to my hearts delight.

These scenarios describe a pretty good perimeter and zone architecture. If I try to jump through the ticket booths, there are enough security guards on hand to tackle me and throw me out. I doubt very many people have succeeded in "climbing the fence" in a modern ball park. The perimeter is fairly secure. Add to that any rogue elements I might be carrying in my bag. While the security check is not optimum, it is effective.

Once inside, I might be able to sneak into the box seats down on the first tier until the real owner of those tickets tells me to get out. Then the usher comes along and tells me to go upstairs where my section is. If I keep trying to sit in a better section but do not have the proper ticket, I will eventually be thrown out of the park. This is a good example of the theory of zone security.

The perimeter of a network is the first point of entry at the demarcation and the first screening hardware found in the server room. This could be a simple router with access control lists. It could be a firebox, a piece of networking hardware with vendor specific firmware that serves as a gate for authenticating users outside of the system and blocking specific kinds of activity. There is also software that is installed in either the router or the server that is referred to as a firewall.

In any given organization there can be any number of perimeters. For business reasons, separate access lines can be installed for specific activity. In a University, I might bring in one or more access lines to the demarcation point for student access to the internet. One may be specifically designated for wireless activity. I might bring in one or more lines for academic access, and then one or more lines to specifically serve the business needs of the university. Each of these access lines could be treated separately with their own firebox, firewall, access controlled router or switch. This effectively separates business functions completely. The students would never see the networks serving the academic side or business networks.

This kind of architecture begins to define what has loosely been referred to as DMZs. This term comes from military jargon; there remains a De-militarized Zone separating North from South Korea; a zone filled with land mines and with large guns focused on it, but no one is allowed inside the zone unless both sides of the conflict agree there is a need. The concept is applied to networks in various ways and administrators refer to this as a DMZ; they separate various servers or segments of a network from the typical user. In our university scenario, the business servers containing all of financial and compliance data of the school would probably be behind a DMZ where only a few top level administrators would have access.

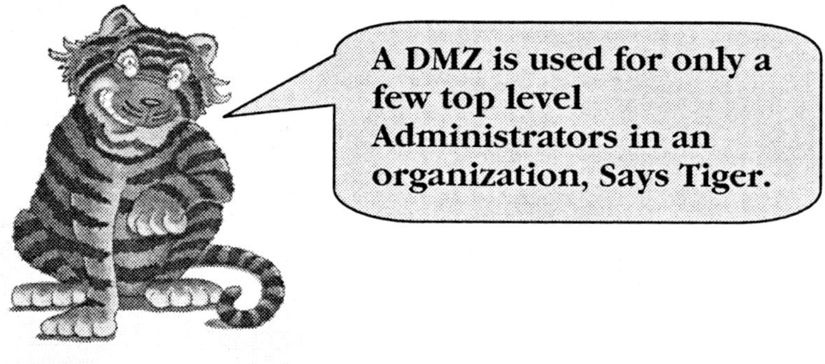

There is no one way to design a secure perimeter. Certain principles can be applied, and there may be budget constraints, but a perimeter can be as secure as an organization desires. The perimeter security is good for keeping external problems out of the system. However, my theory is that this solves only fifteen percent of the problem at best.

Next, there can be any combination of routers, switches, bridges and hubs that begin to divide the network into specific zones. As well, server operating systems such as Unix, Linux or Windows can be configured into zones based on levels of access needed and such things as subnets. These are internal and inside of the perimeter. Dividing an internal system into zones has been effective in segregating most users into their appropriate areas of concern and responsibility. This works for most employees or users who diligently go to work each day to do a good job and do not stray into areas that do not concern them. If they cannot see a server containing sensitive data in their internal browser, they probably will not attempt to access it. A zone can be easily configured to hide segments of the network. If they can see the server and they know access is not allowed, most do not try.

So far what zone security has done is keep out the honest people. Perimeter security has effectively kept out external malicious attacks, viruses, spybots and other undesirables. What has not been effectively addressed in this discussion on perimeter and zone security is the unauthorized user and the rogue element. Let's combine the thinking from Chapter 10 with this discussion.

I recommend administrators rethink the concept of a pure external perimeter and precise internal zones. Taking on the problems of unauthorized internal access and rogue elements requires us to see the inside as having multiple perimeters and the external as potentially being divided into several zones. People who plan physical security for elected officials can teach us something. If I want to meet the President of the United States, I am going to pass through multiple zones, crossing security perimeters at each zone and maybe even multiple perimeters at each edge of a zone until I finally stand in the Oval Office and shake his hand.

Applying this principle to a secure computing environment might be configured so there are different authenticating servers for every zone I want to enter. There might be internal firewalls or fire boxes at every zone edge. A good password policy for this type of environment might be to require a different password for every authenticating server, and perhaps even a different naming convention for every perimeter checkpoint. Inside the routers, there could then still be more access control lists that are specific to user and to MAC address. Further still there could be an application keeping constant vigil over the entire network looking for elements not previously authenticated to the system, isolating them and if they cannot be validated, and perhaps permanently blocking access from all zones.

Effective security of the perimeters and zones requires careful thought. I could give you a recipe here for specific configurations but it may not serve your purposes. Perhaps you have a web server where you are hosting a wiki community where you desire users to enter data and alter the site at will. Extremely tight perimeter and zone security might not be the effective answer. However, the configuration I noted in the previous paragraph might be the foundation of a system holding research and development data for special weapons. And, even as tight as it may seem, it might still require more layers of security.

Finally, the more connections a system has both internally and externally the more risk there is. A computer standing alone inside a locked closet inside the locked office of the owner that has no internet access and no external connections to any other computer and is accessed only by the owner is a fairly secure system. It might not be a practical system for most business needs, but it is secure behind a physical perimeter and within a locked, fire-proof zone. The one user account on the computer has a weird naming convention and a multiple character password. This is the computer I use for my finances.

All of this is moot in an atmosphere of slack management. I have seen complex perimeter and zone security configured to keep an airtight network only to find the server room door unlocked, (and in one case no door on the server room at all) and passwords scribbled on the wall. If this is your idea of a "casual working environment", don't bother with security.

As we move into the next topic, it will become apparent more complex security of computer networks requires fully integrated thinking. As we discuss Extranets, Intranets and Web Portals, we will need to consider these in light of Access Control and Perimeter/Zone security.

Chapter 12

Securing VPNs, Extranets and Intranets

Chapter Objectives

- Understand unique challenges of securing information extranets
- VPNs are valuable, but need special security attention
- Distributed applications offer unique challenges
  - o Especially if they are accessed over a wireless network
  - o If the authentication is poorly managed
- Understand that VPNs and Extranets expand the perimeter to the furthest point accessible.
- Encryption is an easy concept to understand, but may be difficult to implement

Extranets and Intranets are used to disseminate information directly to employees through company controlled web sites that cannot be viewed by persons outside of the company. The distinction between the two is not necessarily important for our purposes here, but who can access them and data security is important. Virtual Private Networks (VPNs) are used to allow direct remote access to the network.

Accessing these whether inside the main office where the servers reside or from a remote location whether it is company owned or just a local coffee shop presents some unique security challenges. My current company email account is accessible from anywhere I have a network connection. The sites governed by the company for internal use might contain data that is considered a trade secret or that is sensitive to national security or is of a personal nature. It is relatively easy to share the drawings for the fighter jet with qualified viewers. Distributed applications especially in design and drafting allow multiples user to view and manipulate drawings at the same time. This might be an extremely efficient way of doing business, but the risk lies in giving access to the wrong person.

The technology underlying the type of extranet that allows multiple users to access data simultaneously finds it roots in early internet broadcasting. Multiple connections are allowed to the source of the data. The IP and MAC addresses of authenticated users are queued and each connection receives the data simultaneously by blending in the server. Early experiments in video chat rooms that allowed up to sixteen users to see and hear each other proved that consistent bandwidth of the users was key to ensuring the experience was the same for all participants. Users with very low dial up bandwidth complained that the data was coming too slow and they missed a lot of the video or the audio portions. People with fiber optic connections complained there was often a two or three minute delay in a response from another user with the slow bandwidth.

It was easier to implement this technology in a tightly controlled corporate environment if the bandwidth to all locations was consistent. An example of this is the Boeing 7e7. Designers involved in the project resided in several different parts of the world and could, at a designated time, meet virtually to discuss extremely sensitive details about the new jet.

In addition to the need for maintaining sound access control mechanisms, the protocols for much of this technology are of concern. Much like chat, if any one of the participants was using a wireless connection that was not fully encrypted, someone could easily intercept the text and even the graphics portions of the session. Once the data flows out of the corporate web server to the participants, their individual locations become perimeters. The extranet has virtually extended the perimeter of the network as far as the most remote participant.

The VPN is an address based direct connection between a remote computer and specific hardware assets on the network. At face value, the connection is nothing more than a stateful session between two designated ports. The vpn configuration software the is embedded in an operating system like Windows establishes a direct, stateful connection between the two computers once an IP and MAC address are entered. When it is activated, the connection is good until it is proactively closed. This is basically the same type of connection used for chat sessions but using a different protocol. If the data passed through the VPN is not hidden in some way, anyone who can sniff this connection can read the data. VPNs are fairly secure when we are dealing with honest people. They are not secure if we are victim to port scans, vampire taps, session hijacking or if the VPN session is improperly configured and unauthorized users are connected.

The VPN was designed to give direct access to specific assets or data. A network administrator could easily access certain servers and remotely manage or monitor activity. Someone in Finance could access specific folders while on a business trip and generate reports. This ability has become a staple of every sized business. Remote access is essential.

Both scenarios of a shared Extranet or a direct Virtual Private Network between a remote computer and networked resources demonstrate two things. First, technological advances often outpace security. As carefully as we plan to secure a new technology someone will attempt to circumvent the security to illicitly access data and assets. Second, new technologies demand a rethinking of access control methods and they extend the perimeter of the network to distances we never planned on.

A response to this seems relatively simple and it is. Encrypt the data. The concept is easy; modify the data somehow at one end using a secret key, share the key with only trusted computers or individuals who can use it to decrypt the data at the other end. It takes a good mathematician to create the encryption methods and secret keys, but it doesn't take much to understand how it works and why we need it.

Encrypting data transmitted by an extranet or across a vpn is handled nicely by third party products or through various new technologies. One method for securing vpns is based on a simple concept; multi protocol label switching. Using switches rather than routers, labels are placed on the data packets that encrypt them and they are sent to specific MAC addresses entered into the configuration. The recipient has the private key and decrypts the data. Switches are known as fast devices because they send data directly to a specific MAC address rather than through access control lists in a router and then through a polling process in a hub. The encrypted data arrives exactly at the MAC address and is quickly decrypted.

While this type of security, which is replicated in various ways by other hardware and software manufacturers, is secure at face value, never lose sight of the problems of illicit access to a system, social engineering and careless configuration. Some perpetrators are extremely patient and wait for opportunities to arise. They wait until there is an opening and capitalize on it.

Chapter 13

Implementing System Monitoring

Chapter Objectives

- System monitoring is essential
- Three specific types of monitoring must be conducted
  - ✓ Performance of the system
  - ✓ External threats to the system
  - ✓ Internal threats to the system
- Performance monitoring reveals potential risk to actual transmission
- External monitoring reveals port scanning, sniffing and virus threats
- Internal monitoring reveals illicit/illegal attempts by users to access data

System monitoring is as important as flossing your teeth. How many administrators do you think floss their teeth every day? In this chapter, I want to divide the subject of monitoring into three distinct types of monitoring, each equally important. First, administrators monitor for performance, then there is pro active monitoring of external attacks at the perimeter and finally, and often more importantly, there is a need to actively monitor users inside the system.

Each type of monitoring uses different tools and the results of the monitoring are interpreted differently. Performance is typically a mechanical issue; are all of the essential distribution nodes plugged in turned on and functional and are all cables passing data? External threats are monitored at the point of entry using routers, switches, fireboxes and firewalls. Internal monitoring of users sadly is not readily supported with application tools. The reason for this is the demand for tools has been for performance and external threat monitoring.

I learned details of an incident where a sensitive server was compromised and client data was copied and also stolen. The loss was multifaceted. There were costs associated with the actual loss of the data which caused an interruption in regular business activity. There were costs associated with restoring the data, much of which was not backed up. There were costs associated with loss of trust with major clients. Finally there was the cost of the investigation.

I am not privy to all of the details of the case, and shouldn't be. But, what was clear was the incident was perpetrated by someone inside the system. The access control was not properly configured and a user accessed the data files.

I asked if there was a key logging or other type of monitoring system in place. There was not. They didn't log access attempts to any of the data files. I am not sure if the police were able to charge anyone in the incident, but the administrators of that system decided they needed another level of security. The only monitoring system in place was for performance and a passive monitoring of intrusions at the perimeter. There was no internal monitoring of user activity.

Whenever I raise the issue of user monitoring, many people seem to focus on illicit or even illegal internet activity. If a user policy expressly prohibits specific activity, then user monitoring will consider this aspect. There are third party applications that will list URLs, the web site name. More sophisticated applications can actually replicate content into a log file. Windows administrators can easily capture history of internet usage and view thumbnail images of the type of content viewed. I used one or all of these methods when it was deemed important by policy to monitor internet activity. It is not a pleasant task, however, and one that junior administrators tire of quickly.

User monitoring, however, should focus on the files, folders, directories, drives and servers users can or attempt to access. Once decisions are made about the level of access for each user, the configuration of permissions requires careful attention as noted before in this book; permissions can migrate across an Enterprise if they are not configured correctly.

Budgetary constraints are often cited as the primary reason for not pro-actively monitoring user activity. In many of these cases, however, time and resources are deployed to monitor external attacks against systems that have already been hardened. External monitoring has cache; the trusted network administrator is seen as the gate keeper protecting all and everything on the inside.

Internal monitoring is not popular. Tracking what people do once they are hired and logged into a system always raises privacy issues. People do not like the concept of big brother watching. Even if there is full disclosure of monitoring during the hiring process, employees still complain. Managers have to balance this anxiety with what I have stated repeatedly in this book that usually 85% of security problems are inside the system.

I tried to convince one junior administrator of this and to get him focused on internal threats. Instead, he spent his time monitoring external pings and the port scans launched against his system. I asked if this external activity succeeded in penetrating the system or revealing any pertinent security information. He proudly said no, it had not; he had the perimeter locked down fairly tightly. I then pointed out that during my system assessment, I discovered that everyone in the company had access to the folder containing information about the impending Initial Public Offering. The data had been copied but there was no log of users who had gained access to the folder. This was potentially a serious violation of the Security and Exchange Commission laws governing the public offering of company stock. In my security analysis report, I fully identified that the external perimeter was fairly secure but there was no internal security of the most sensitive data.

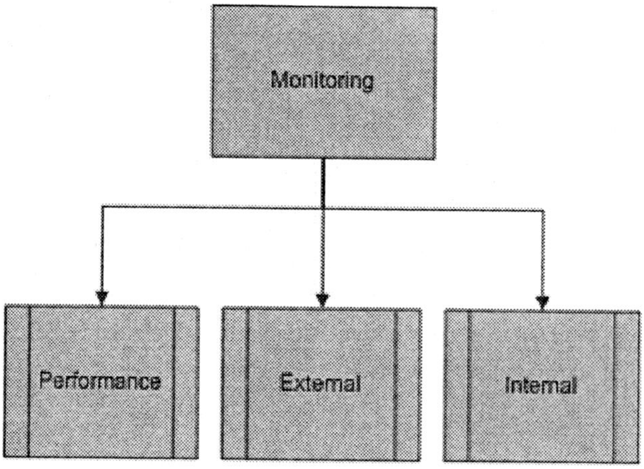

Here is a check list of basic items and activity that should be monitored on a regular basis. There are several third party applications that will easily handle any one of these monitoring activities:

Performance

System Through-put: What is the total capacity of data through-put of the system and are there any breaks or bottle necks.

Quality of Service: (QoS) When there is scheduled demand for bandwidth dedication for the transfer of sensitive or large amounts of data, monitor the system prior to and during the scheduled transfer to ensure adequate QoS.

Node Capacity: Monitor the processes on mission critical nodes (router, switch, bridge, firebox, server) to ensure adequate system hardware for critical demands.

Rogue elements or unknown nodes: Check to see if a computer or wireless device not belonging to the organization has been given access to network services and access.

Vampire Taps: These may not be caught by electronic monitoring so it might be necessary to visually inspect cabling from the demarcation point to the server.

External Monitoring

Port Scans: Monitor all attempted port scans and gather source data of the scanner.

Viruses, Bots, Rootkits and Trojans: Monitor all incoming data including data transfers, attachments, email messages and chat sessions at the point of entry for any malicious code.

Remote Access: Monitor all remote access attempts. Log all attempts whether successful or not. Monitor and log all valid and illicit user names, password crack attempts and all successful and unsuccessful password attempts.

Remote Access Activity: Monitor and log all remote access activity. This should include all file, folder, director and drive access.

Internal Monitoring

Data Access: Monitor and log all access attempts to sensitive data. This data can be used later to determine legitimate or illicit access.

Log Ins: Monitor and log all log ins. Employees are fairly habitual about times when they start and stop work. Anomalous activity may point to identity spoofing or illicit log in attempts.

Internal Virus Infections: Monitor all internal traffic for the introduction of Viruses, bots, rootkits and trojans from user owned and transferred storage devices.

Internet Activity: If there is a policy in place, monitor internet traffic for compliance.

Changes to Data: Differential back up reports can identify any changes made to archived data. For the purpose of claiming archived data has integrity, it is necessary to know if someone has, for any good or bad reason, altered data that has been stored. Yes, this means conducting a differential back up of data that has already been backed up.

Systematic Analysis of Access Permissions: Hold managers accountable by asking who has access to various levels of data and compare that to permissions set in the network operating system.

Chapter 14:

Implementing Back Up, Storage and Recovery Procedures

Chapter Objectives

- Backing up data is an essential function
- There are three types of back ups
  - Incremental, Differential and Full
- Administrators should also do "day zero" back ups of new systems
- Data should be duplicated and stored off site in climate controlled areas
- Data restoration plans should be in place and practiced

My mother used to say it was a good thing I didn't have a twin; two of me would be too much. I can't say the same thing about data. Having two or three exact copies of every important piece of data is essential.

While I was in school completing a Masters degree, I was working for a virtual library managing their Linux download center. Fellow classmates knew I was handy with a computer and when they would lose or corrupt an important paper really late the night before it was due, I would get the call. They wanted me to perform magic and get the paper back to its original condition. All I could usually ask was if they had backed up a copy and they always said no. I enjoyed a night cap, placed two copies of my papers in my folio, backed up my electronic versions and went to bed. Some of these folks actually learned to back up important data.

An administrator responsible for a large data farm regularly backed up his servers and placed them in a basement room rather than wait until 5:00 p.m. for the off site storage van to arrive. Of course the basement flooded and three years of data tapes sat under four feet of water for several days. Very little of the data could be recovered.

As I mentioned in the preface of this book, a few astute financial investment firms located in the World Trade Center were operational the week after the incident. This was partly due to the topics I will cover in Chapter 16, but as importantly due to the regular and safe back up and storage of all data. I was particularly happy with one company; they managed my meager investments.

Back Ups

The principles of data back ups is easy. There are Incremental, Differential and Full Back Ups. Some administrators do not implement differential back ups and are satisfied with incremental and full. The differences between incremental and differential are subtle; incremental catches all data added or changed after the last incremental back up. The differential catches all changes to existing data after a full back up. The full back up, of course, is just that. Also, a good practice is to back up the system using what is called a day zero back up, or backing up the entire system as it stood the day it was installed. For static systems that will not change much over the span of a year or two, this is helpful to have in the event there is a catastrophic system failure.

Most administrators run incremental back ups on weekday nights after normal operations and then a full back up on a weekend night. Back up applications can easily be configured to run automatically and no one really needs to be present at the time of the back up. This strategy will change for operations that are 24/7 services. In these cases, administrators look for time frames of least activity and run their back ups during then. Some data might not be caught during the back up if there is a stateful session of data entry, but it will be caught during the next back up session. This situation might call for daily incremental and full back ups.

Data can be backed up on to a variety of media ranging from floppies, which make almost no sense except for the causal home users up to very expensive tape magnetic tape drives, which are usually the preferred media of data farms. Many small companies use CDRW or DVDR disks, but this can be a cumbersome method. Smaller, less expensive DAT magnetic tape drives interface nicely with back up applications and administrators run the back ups off hours or remotely and then simply make a physical tape change in the server room the next day.

When I serve as an administrator, I make full back ups typically every day. This adds some expense to the tape budget, but I have never been caught without a copy of important data. I prefer magnetic tapes because the application interface assumes this media and the configuration of the back up rotation is easy.

There is no excuse for not having a copy of important data. As I write this guide book, I make a full back up of the book every time I make a change. There is little need to archive versions, so I keep only those duplicate copies required by the publisher.

Data Storage

Storing archived data becomes a little tricky. The mantra is the data must be kept Confidential, it must be Available and it must have Integrity. Simply put, only authorized personnel should have access, it must be available when needed, and it must be the data that was sent for archiving and was not changed or corrupted after being sent.

There are two primary considerations when planning on storing archived data. First, what media is going to be used, that is will it be stored on floppies, zip drives, remote hard drives, CDRWs or magnetic tape. To be considered are cost, efficieny storage space required and the longevity of the media. Second, where is the best place to store it and still honor the need for Confidentiality, Availability and Integrity.

Magnetic tapes last longer if they are stored in cool, dark and dry rooms that are under constant climate control. They don't last long if they are thrown in a box and stuffed in damp, overheated crawl spaces. Data is subject to theft if it is not stored in very secure rooms. Imagine a company spending thousands monitoring for active data theft from a server and then throwing back up tapes in a drawer accessible to all employees. The person who does this knows who he is and should be embarrassed or fired.

It is possible to reduce data storage costs by reducing the amount of data that goes to storage. Make sure all parties know exactly what data must be stored. In addition to normal business operations, there are federal, state and local regulations governing the storage of data depending on the type of operation. Medical and student records must be stored for specific amounts of time and easily recoverable by governing bodies. Documents sensitive to police investigations must be stored as long as the court says they must.

While cost cutting is important, consider the cost of re-structuring data from hard copy files because the proper methods, media and location were minimized. We would never want the police to subpoena files, but they may have a reason to do so and they want the complete files. Aside from the politics of complying with the subpoena, as administrators we want to provide the complete files and management can play politics with them if they want.

It is advisable to consider outsourcing storage of data. There are reputable data storage facilities used by major corporations in every city. At some expense, they provide climate controlled, physically secure storage and retrieval services. The data is usually available on demand at the facility or can be delivered. Many offer remote access to the data. Don't cheap out and use the attic or a leaky basement for data storage.

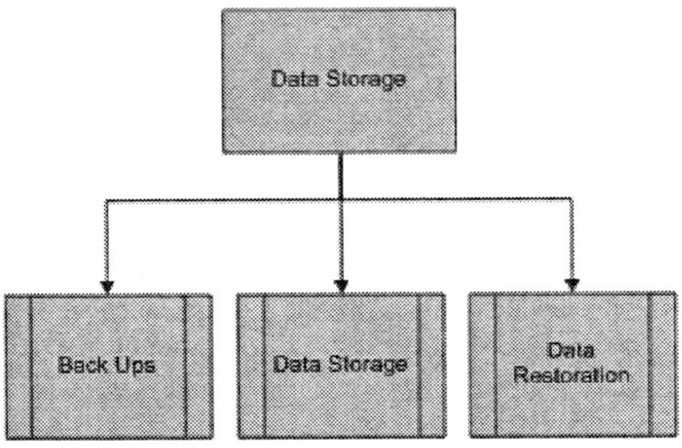

Data Restoration

In the last chapter of this book, we will discuss various strategies for making sure business operations are not interrupted in the event of a catastrophe. In this final section of this chapter, let's focus on making sure we know how to restore data from archived copies.

Most data archiving applications have a restore option. This option assumes a data back up tape, hard drive or

CDRW is present and the restoration process is fairly straight forward. That is if the administrator has practiced.

I want to assume the worst case scenario in any situation I take over. After making my assessment of the system, I look for the archived data storage and learn the naming conventions of the data files. I then set about the process of finding surplus hardware and creating a test environment for catastrophe. First, I sabotage data bases, then I corrupt the files with viruses and attack the system with Denial of Service attacks and finally I just cut and paste (nice way of saying 'steal') sensitive data. I then retrieve the latest back ups from storage and restore the environment to its original condition. Or, the condition I can achieve given the type of back up, the integrity of the data, the availability of the media, the condition of the media, the climate in the storage facility and the documented restoration process.

Only once in the ten times I completed this type of emergency response test was I able to replicate the original environment. That was not because of lack of skill. I worked with some of the brightest individuals who cared deeply for the quality of their administrative services. Budget cuts, however, often dictated the type of back ups run, media used, storage facilities accessed and I can guarantee the less consideration given to these, there was a corresponding lack of quality in the restoration. This is not important until the hurricane takes out your data center and you have customers trying to access their accounts.

Document the emergency response test. Find out if this condition is acceptable to senior management. If not, find the cause for any break down in the back up and storage system and correct it. Run the test again until the results are acceptable.

Backing up and safely archiving data is not just something that is mentioned at the end of a book on network security. It is one of the most vital functions of the network administrator and if every over looked should be the end of that person's job.

Chapter 15:

Rotating Responsibilities and Auditing the Admnistrator

Chapter Objectives

- Everyone who uses or manages a network is accountable
- Even the administrator must be audited
- It is essential to rotate duties and audit
- Implement rotation of duties carefully in a professional manner
- Understand that even good people can become corrupt

I have a friend with a wicked sense of humor; he has a degree in accounting. Instead of throwing crude, common expletives at each other, preferably while flashing the middle finger, we use a different expression. We look at each other and just simply say "audit you". That expression is worse than any other crude expression.

A complete information security program mandates accountability. The user is accountable to the supervisor and the administrator is seen and the objective reporter of activity. The supervisor is accountable ultimately to the owner of the company, whether and individual or a board of directors. The board is accountable to the stock holders. The network administrator is ultimately accountable to every level of governance. No one is exempt. A network administrator who behaves as if he is needs to be removed.

Old school administrators like to posit themselves as the end of the road; they have the final say. They do not. In a good security program, administrators rotate their responsibilities especially as it pertains to accessing and protecting sensitive information. The administrator who takes over from the previous is tasked with auditing. The rotation of responsibility can be planned or randomly applied. If you want to ensure security, select the random method.

A large corporation in Seattle was able to identify the theft and sale of trade secrets by rotating responsibilities and auditing their network administrators. A network administrator is able to orchestrate events that are almost undetectable. Until they are thoroughly audited, these events may occur for years without any detection.

If there is a small IT department and rotation is not feasible, there are accounting firms who specialize in auditing IT administrators, systems and processes. This is a different service from a security scan where the consultant may conduct an external penetration test or an internal access control test. This is specifically designed to determine if the network administrator is working to secure the network or participating in illicit or illegal practices using the company networking assets.

These practices are not perfect. It is possible for administrators, security officers and auditors to collude and perpetrate crimes almost without detection. Also, auditing perfectly honest administrators can affect positive morale in the short run. No professional likes to think of themselves as being under investigation. However, everyone is ultimately accountable and no one is above the law. If a system has allowed an administrator to operate with impunity, the opportunity for corruption increases.

I noted briefly a story in the beginning of this book about a school where the administrator befriended college age students in what I saw as an unethical manner. Rather than developing collegial working relationships with peers, he spent his social and professional time with students. He became disgruntled with the school management and ultimately found himself being reprimanded for a number of code of conduct violations. It was clear that the progressive discipline would eventually catch up to him because he was determined not to change his behavior. He resigned but not before poisoning the students attitudes toward the school and giving them a key to the server room and all administrative passwords. Before they were able to perpetrate any kind of crime, an astute administrator had the locks changed and a new administrator immediately changed all access passwords.

A programmer with access to source code of completed projects colluded with an administrator and between the two of them they sold millions of dollars worth of popular software for their personal financial gain. This activity went undetected for years and was discovered only when some of the software did not function correctly and the help desk noticed the CD Keys were identical to those belonging to a company who had legally purchased the application. The network administrator was a very trusted and long standing friend of the owner.

Rotating responsibilities and auditing powerful administrators does not need to foster a climate of fear and retribution. Professionals understand accountability. Introducing the concept in a professional, collegial manner is necessary. Where there is fear, there will be lost productivity. People will spend time documenting and proving their innocence rather than working. But to ignore the power of the network administrator especially around sensitive and valuable information is simply irresponsible.

Another strategy might mitigate hard feelings. It is commonly known as Segregation of Duties. It is the same concept as the control mechanisms in place for launching a nuclear weapon. There are codes and physical keys held by separate and unrelated individuals and all of them must enter their code or key in exactly the precise order, each one verifying if the command is legitimate. This serves to ensure that there are no rogue elements unilaterally trying to start a nuclear war.

In a network environment, multiple administrators have varying responsibilities. One might be responsible for daily log maintenance. One might have access to the data in the database, but not the access control logs. Another might manage a log that records log in attempts and data access attempts. This type of system is not intended to create snitches but it is intended to reduce the opportunity for internal malicious behavior on the part of the administrators.

Most people take great pride in their work and do not want to be associated with illicit or illegal activity. The thought of jail time is not a pleasant one. They bring to the job an attitude of caring, professionalism and diligence. That is until they are in need and the opportunity for quick gain arises, or until they are treated poorly and have total control of valuable electronic assets. And there are sloppy, incompetent administrators who have complete control and fail to notice illegal activity, such as the one administrator who allowed some illegal pornography to go unnoticed on his server simply because he was too lazy to audit. He served time for his laziness.

Good people can and will turn bad. Bad people will simply find opportunity. Managers do a service to employees by creating an environment that reduces opportunity for illicit and illegal activity. Creating a network environment where all are equally accountable and duties are rotated and segregated serves this purpose well.

Chapter 16:

Designing Secure, Scalable Systems

Chapter Objectives

- Network systems must be both secure and scalable
- Security should be at the core of the scalable plan
- To begin, understand what the business does and build an appropriate system
- Understand centralized and de-centralized management philosophies
- Understand the unique needs of software and hardware infrastructures
- Be diligent in securing a growing system

Up to this point in the book, I have assumed an administrator is taking over an existing network system. Starting with the assessment and ending with data restoration, the system pre-existed and the administrator needed to rectify where the system was not functional or where is was vulnerable.

Assume for this chapter the building you will occupy is a concept in the architect's mind and you have been invited to speak to issues pertaining to the computer network. Assume also it is a well funded start up and the plan for the first year is to develop operations at headquarters and then over five years expand to five states and three countries. Within ten years, the corporation will be a truly global enterprise. But, today, the architect has a sketch pad and some bright ideas from your CEO.

My first questions are simple. What do we do? Do we retail toys? Do we make bombs for the Air Force? Do we provide medical care to indigent peoples? Do we have the world's largest chain of discount department stores? Are we a research institute with a lot of intellectual property and the need to process complex calculations? I have given very divergent examples to illustrate that computing needs are as divergent as these organizations and therefore the architecture of the system and the security needs are going to be equally divergent. Starting with a packaged solution simply will not work.

I enjoyed a television commercial several years ago about financial planning services claiming to be customized to individual needs. The financial planner listened to a doctor about his income and retirement needs and gave him Plan A. He then listened to the grade school teacher and gave her Plan A, and so on. I have seen too many pre-packed sales presentations from hardware and software vendors to start there. They do not answer my questions or respond individually to my needs.

On the other hand, I have been brought in to consult in situations where no real planning had taken place and then a barely adequate network was retrofitted as demand grew. A large social service organization implemented a Metropolitan Area Network (MAN) after installing very different LAN architectures in several satellite offices. While each unit manager was on board to unify the network, no planning had gone into the initial investment of hardware and software. The result was an expensive retrofit that did not function well.

There are philosophical differences driven by the peculiarities of business drivers. One CEO of an investment company was adamant the system would be easy for him to use from home. Another business owner only cared about having cameras over the cash registers so he could watch transactions take place in his fifteen locations. One director of a school required only that he could watch the hallways remotely from home to see if his instructors were providing education to students for all of the required hours. After that, none of these three business decisions makers claimed to care a lot about the security of the systems, but invested little or no time in guiding the process.

There are several competing philosophies regarding the design of large scale, wide area networks. There are even more competing philosophies for securing them. As technologies evolve, so do these philosophies. Rather than recommend adoption of any one of them, I want to sort them out and apply them to specific needs.

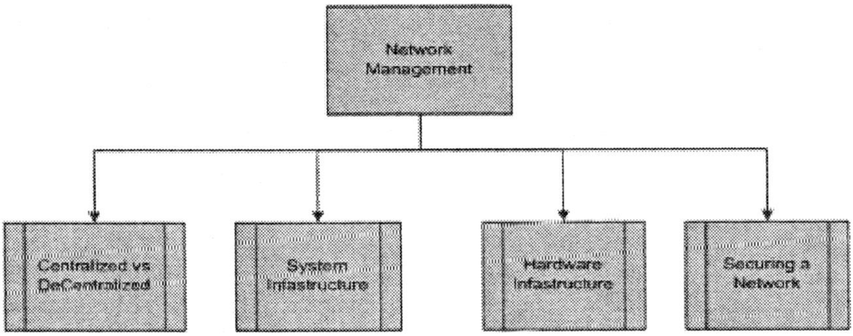

I start this consideration of network design with this caveat; the system must serve the business needs of the organization, not the desires and fantasies of the network administrator. The data, services and their security come first. Secondly, once the architecture serves the business model, it should be planned to adapt and scale up for growth. Buying a network architecture for a projected five or ten year growth pattern is usually a waste of money. Good businesses adapt to the economy and to growth. They scale according to the movements of the economy. Bad network planning and investments plagued the telecommunications industry. I know of buildings full of unused networking equipment that anticipated wild growth in land line telephone service and did not adapt to the growth in cell phone use.

Centralized Vs. De-centralized Control

First, let's discuss the difference between centralized and decentralized network management. In a large, global WAN with multiple business units, the debate over this rages constantly. Large networks serving different business units within the same geographical area, such as a university, engage in this debate as well. Where the owner of the network stands on this issue will drive the design.

Centralized control usually consists of one main location of business servers for data storage, email, remote access services, internet access and other business functions. Remote locations might be equipped with authentication and print servers for local usage. This is an extreme form of centralization where all applications are distributed and users are really working over a secure network on a server at the central location. The remote locations require very little administration. Users can be added remotely from the central office and print drivers can be managed either remotely or on site by relatively inexperienced network personnel.

In this model, data might be entered directly into central data bases as users work, or it might be held in the remote server until the end of the work day and sent to the central location at night.

Working with distributed applications that enter data real time from the remote location into central data bases might require the purchase of more bandwidth, or dedicated bandwidth. The more people using the application the more bandwidth required to speed up the process. If the data is entered and stored locally, a system will need to be designed to hold the data, back it up locally as required and then to successfully transmit the data to the central data bases at a specified time.

There are several benefits to centralized management if it serves the business needs of the organization. These include one point of entry and filtering of internet access; one depository of data or centrally managed depositories of data; one centrally managed security system for access controls, authentication and monitoring; the ability to monitor and update workstations remotely from one location. The disadvantages to centralized management include: the system is rigid and it can be slow to respond to local needs; there is little or no local control of desktop applications; the larger the organization, the longer it takes to set up new employees; local equipment failure or installation may require expensive outsourced service; the services offered to local users may be limited to the shared applications.

Decentralized management might be a combination of several architectures and even different operating system platforms. The architecture can be as granular as every server is in a standalone Local Area Network (LAN) with a connecting backbone to all other LANs on the system. Each server would require an administrator for all work and it would be done locally. An extreme form of this might be a collection of independent networks connecting several small stores where each store is required to install and manage applications, maintain all data, administer any internet connections, monitor all traffic, create user accounts and repair/install all equipment locally.

The advantages of having total local control in a decentralized system include: Quick response to local issues, assuming a qualified network administrator is on site; Independent operations that are responsive to local needs; the ability to segregate networks and responsibilities so no one network or person has control of all operations; localized management of security. The disadvantages would be: Little or no sharing and therefore reduction in cost of system wide services; Isolated data bases that would require consolidation; Little control of organizational user policies; Little or no ability to leverage system wide purchases; Fragmented and localized security monitoring.

Somewhere in between these extremes is a combination of centralized and localized management that serves specific business needs. Let's look at how they could be applied to various business models.

In a privately owned school system with numerous campuses nationwide where the curriculum and degree offerings are basically the same throughout, the centralized model may be a better fit. All of the data gathered about the student from enrollment through financial aid up to grades and finally granting a degree must be held in one central database. By federal law, this data must be secured so no personal information about the student can be accessible to anyone not having a legitimate role in the school. By utilizing a system of centrally managed distributed applications, students can get information about the school, apply, enroll, finance, take courses, receive grades and new schedules and finally graduate. Staff and faculty log into a system, launch the application interface and all details about the student's activity at the school is populating the central data base in real time. The local network is easily managed mostly with remote access, but student assistance is utilized for local installation and maintenance. The local server is used for authentication and shared print drivers. This system exists and is effective, yet with some downside; some of the applications are not optimized for the system and can be irritatingly slow. Also, knowing there could be an interruption in device, data is held locally for some applications and sent directly to the central database at random times throughout the night. In this instance, centralization works.

Another organization owns twenty retail outlets in six states. The outlets serve a local customer and little if any of the goods are replicated across the stores. Really the only thing in common is the owner. There is no need for internet access. There is only a need for local inventory control, financial accounting and payroll. Financial data is sent redundantly on CD ROMs and entered at the owner's office into a centralized data base. There was an effort to plan and cost out a fully inter connected network with a mix of centrally managed databases for finances, but local control of inventory. The cost of this far outweighed the financial benefit and the enterprise remains at twenty standalone LANs.

What should be clear now is the owner of a networked system can have as much or little centralized control as required for the business model. This has only effectively evolved over the past ten years for every type of business model. Only the very large and wealthy corporations could afford to implement any distributed but centrally managed services, and even these were arcane in comparison to what is now available.

System Infrastructure

Once a management model is chosen for the architecture this will begin to dictate the infrastructure of the data communications. This means the architecture will now dictate the bandwidth required.

Beginning with selecting bandwidth and therefore dictating architecture is a very old school method; one that assumes the Plain Old Telephone Service (POTS) is the only cost effective means of interconnecting networks. This mentality of network planning had the network architecture being subservient to available bandwidth. Now, the wide variety of data communications capabilities serves the systems architects who can plan and implement pretty much any system they choose, selecting the appropriate bandwidth after the most suitable architecture is chosen. There are a few minor exceptions still in this country to that, but they are really few in number.

Cost may be a limiting factor. Once an architecture is chosen, the appropriate bandwidth, while available, my not make economic sense. The architects revisit the plan and produce a balanced system that satisfies data delivery needs and budget constraints. They scale back the services, knowing more can be added back later. The architects now have an adaptive scalable plan that allows them to roll out more services across the system as bandwidth becomes more cost effective.

Hardware infrastructure

In my administrative roles, I was inundated with advertising for muscle hardware. It didn't matter what size of enterprise I was associated with, I got advertising for bigger, faster and more powerful hardware. This is an area where many architects simply waste money. Instead of starting with a consideration of the business model that must be served and planning an adaptive and scalable system around that, they begin with hardware. Too many times I see very expensive hardware serving a handful of users when it was designed to handle thousands of remote users and terrabytes of data. If there is money to burn in an IT department, it usually ends up in hardware.

I am amused when a business owner is caught up in the showmanship of owning the most powerful router on the market to serve fifty employees. I was given a tour of a start up with twenty people. The CEO bragged he had spent over five hundred thousand dollars on a network. I worked in a consulting capacity for a while, recommending they shed much of the unused networking equipment and instead upgrade the graphics workstations since they were in the graphics design business, not the Enterprise wide networking business. I offered a network design that was scalable to five cities, was mostly centrally controlled and offered a unique opportunity for clients to meet remotely on line in real time with the designers. If they had sold half of the equipment, they could have upgraded the workstations and increased the bandwidth to make this a reality and they had a plan to adapt scale up as needed. The owner instead chose to buy even more equipment as well as the bandwidth in order to have all five cities fully functional. They went broke.

Securing the adaptive and scalable network

If the principles of network security covered in this book are observed, there is little problem adding segments, services or applications to a network that is scaling up. There is an extension in the perimeter, there are more zones, the number of users multiplies and the data traffic increases. The monitoring and incident response capabilities need to scale up as well.

Chapter 17

Planning Effective Disaster Recovery

Chapter Objectives

- Disaster recover plans are essential
- Good disaster recovery planning may require duplicate systems
- The objective is to be operational as quickly as possible to limit loss
- There are seven steps in developing a plan

  ✓ Policy Statement
  ✓ Business Impact Analysis
  ✓ Preventive Controls
  ✓ Contingency Plan
  ✓ Test, train, Practice
  ✓ On-going Plan Maintenance

- The plan will always need revision as business units change focus or grow

In treating this subject, I want to refer to the worst terrorist incident inflicted on this country, what is commonly referred to by its date; 9/11. I use this example out of respect for those who perished, those who suffered injury or loss and those whose economic lives were destroyed or grossly interrupted. The topic of system redundancy could not have saved lives or reduced personal loss or injury, but it did reduce the negative economic impact.

It is speculated the objective of the attacks on the World Trade Center were multifaceted. It is understood that flying an airplane into a tall building is going to inflict death and bodily harm, and doing so at the start of a work day is going to maximize this. But, the World Trade Center was also not only a symbol of capitalism but actually the home of several investment banks, stock brokerage firms, accountants, investment and tax lawyers and other financial professionals. It was de facto a center of capitalism and physically attacking it might have had deep symbolic meaning, but it is clear the objective was also to negatively impact the economy as much as possible.

If all of the computer systems in the World Trade Center were not duplicated in some fashion, there would have been a grossly negative impact on the economy. Clear thinking network architecture however resulted in a variety of redundant systems allowing many of those who survived the attack to stand up and go back to work.

Disaster planning is an integral part of system architecting. The goal is to be able to move from a primary network to a back up system quickly if not instantaneously.

Having a tape back up system is a good first step toward a complete disaster recovery plan. The back up tape, however, is not much good unless there is a server to place the data on, workstations to utilize the data in the conduct of business, a network for efficiently sharing data and resources and a physical place for people to work.

The completeness of a recovery plan depends on the importance of the business unit. I would want my bank to recover from a disaster quickly. I would like the local hospital to have systems up and running fast. Police and fire communications networks should also have priority. The website where I play shared games is not that important and that can wait. In fact if that site was permanently down, I wouldn't care much.

There are commonly accepted terms and processes for developing effective recovery plans established by the National Institute of Standards and Technology (NIST) which is part of the Department of Commerce. I will use that framework for the content of this chapter.

The seven steps in the development lifecycle of a recovery plan are:

Contingency and Recovery Policy Statement

Conduct a Business Impact Analysis (BIA)

Identify Preventive Controls

Develop Recovery Strategies

Develop a Contingency Plan for Information Technology

Test, Train and Practice

Implement On-going Plan Maintenance

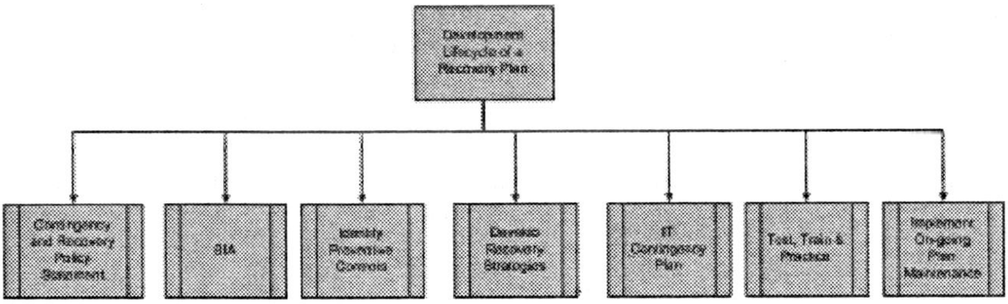

Contingency and Recovery Policy Statement

This serves as a roadmap of what needs to be done in the event of a disaster. The Policy Statement will declare the intent of contingencies and recovery planning; is it the goal of the organization to be immediately functional at whatever cost, or is the goal to exactly duplicate the information technology infrastructure or is the goal to bring the organization back into functionality over an acceptable period of time. This declaration can be whatever the organization wants; just be clear in this goal so the plans developed will actually reflect it. This policy is also an instrument to define levels of authority if any managerial personnel are affected by the disaster. There should be a clear plan for authoritative continuity along with continuity of services.

Conduct a Business Impact Statement

Just as there are various levels of importance in business functions, there are also varying levels of disaster. If the use of the internet is not mission critical, then the BIA should reflect this value and the contingency plan would consider the issue of reestablishing connection to an ISP of lesser importance than perhaps connecting to the data bases. Define the most mission critical systems and services first and the least critical last. Plans should reflect these values. This will help in expediting recovery of the most critical functions.

During the assessment phase found in Chapters 2 & 3, I advised administrators to assess local hazards and rating the potential of these occurring on the business premise. This assessment will be helpful in determining what level of disaster could potentially happen. The plan should always first assume total loss of systems and services and respond accordingly, but should then allow for lower levels of loss. An organization is not going to move all IT operations into new equipment if a water main breaks and damages one of fifteen servers.

A thorough BIA should reflect the dollar value of various levels of loss. This will be helpful in determining the level of response. If there is total loss, there will be a total response. If there is minor loss, the amount budgeted for response should be commensurate with that level of loss.

Identify Preventive Measures

In the assessment phase, we also covered the concept of preparing for disasters in several ways, such as raising computer assets off the floor in flood prone areas and securing equipment racks and equipment in a manner that would mitigate the power of most earthquakes. Those practices and procedures belong here in the Contingency and

Recovery plan. During a regular analysis of the plan, these are checked to ensure preparedness.

The organizational IT Security Plan is part of this section as well. That plan will reflect what is proactively done on a regular basis to prevent external and internal attacks. The measures taken to ensure security will in large measure serve to prevent disasters. The objective is to prevent disaster as much as possible but to have a Disaster Contingency and Recovery Plan in place just in case.

Develop Recovery Strategies

Beginning with a response to total system failure, the strategy will include the personnel, policies and procedures for creating a fully functional system. There are several options when considering the total recovery of a system. There could be an exact duplicate system in place that auto senses when the primary system fails and takes over instantaneously. This is known as a Hot Site. There could also be a system set up in a secure environment that is a pared down version of the primary system where copies of the data back up tapes are stored. The system is not powered, but with minimal effort could be. This is a Cold Site. In between these two scenarios, or in a Warm Site, varying levels of readiness can be achieved. And, depending on the importance of the business unit, the plan could be in place to simply resource hardware and networking connectivity and to rebuild the system in a timely manner.

The type of response will depend on the BIA and the amount of money the organization is willing to budget for disasters. This plan should include all pertinent contact information for technical resources, authority to act, financial resource information for emergency purchases and the names and contact numbers for every functional member of the disaster recovery team.

Develop Contingency Plan for Information Technology

A disaster recovery plan is only as good as the available resources after the disaster. This includes hardware, software, electrical power, network infrastructure, internet connectivity, work space and the people necessary to complete the work and manage the system. Depending on the scope of the disaster, some or all of these resources may need to be replaced.

Contingency plans begin with the most probable disaster of extreme proportions. In parts of California this may be a 9.7 earthquake, or as was witnessed more recently, devastating wild fires. After the 1996 attack on the World Trade Center, contingey plans became very real and immediately following 9/11, to a lesser or greater degree, the plans were effectively implemented. It is difficult to be the person who determines that one type of disaster might result in total devastation of a computer system and the people running them, but that is effective contingency planning.

Contingency planning should incorporate as many potential risks as possible from devastating disasters, through theft of data bases to simple user error resulting in loss of power. The risks are grounded in real potential, such as fires, floods, earthquakes and the like and the real potential of them happening. External or Internal attacks on a system resulting in data loss, system failure or theft are regularly evaluated and prioritized based on system security threats. The contingency plan , then, is a living document that is regularly revisited and revised as necessary.

Test, Train & Practice

Once an initial disaster recovery plan is in place, various response scenarios should be tested. The test should be fully documented beginning with the scenario, the initial response to the incident, whether the response met the desired criteria, if the response was adequate and then fully evaluated for effectiveness. This evaluation then cycles back to the contingency plan to rework any necessary portions of it to improve incident response.

Don't neglect the incident response test. As cumbersome as it might seem, it is as necessary as a fire drill.

Implement On-going Plan Maintenance

For every organization, there should be time set aside on a regular basis for the purpose of testing and evaluating and then revising the disaster recovery plan. Additionally, the entire system is continuously evaluated for risk as new elements are added to business units and old units are closed or sold off. Upgrades in technology are to be evaluated and implemented where it positively affects the plan. Local resources should be constantly evaluated to determine availability of servers, workstations, workspace, infrastructure and internet connections. Service Level Agreements should be evaluated on a regular basis to adjust budgets and to ensure the vendor has contingency plans in the even they are affected by the same disaster.

If a disaster occurs and these planning steps have been managed correctly, the appropriate response will be well rehearsed, the resources available and an action plan in place to restore normal operations as quickly as possible.

Chapter 18

National Industrial Security Program

Chapter Objectives

- Doing business with the Defense Department requires solid security practices
- The Department of Defense must certify network systems for classified data
- The requirements include:
  - ✓ Clearing and sanitizing
  - ✓ Examination of hardware and software
  - ✓ Authentication methods
  - ✓ Maintenance
  - ✓ Malicious Code
  - ✓ Physical Security
  - ✓ Protection of Media
  - ✓ Configuration management
- There are unique protection requirements and protection measures

The need for information security for my collection of recipes is fairly low. In fact, if someone stole them, I wouldn't mind. Systems that support our national security, however, can directly affect the lives of millions of citizens. This is where security really matters.

Aside from the few personalities who aspire to this work because of the inherent power, the people I have met over the decades who are responsible for national security do their jobs out of a sense of loyal patriotism. It is more sacrifice than power trip. To ensure the right people manage the secret information assets belonging to the Department of Defense but are sitting on servers belonging to private contractors, the DoD has written specific guidelines for the safe keeping of that information.

The document known as the National Industrial Security Program Operations Manual (NISPOM) defines in detail the levels of security for employees to determine levels of access as well as the criteria for being certified to house these varying levels of secret information and conduct business with the various agencies of the DoD. It goes on further to define processes and policies necessary for securing these systems.

The focus of the first section of this chapter will be to highlight the important issues necessary to attain the proper level of certification in order to contract with the DoD.

The second section will serve as an overview of the specific security requirements contained in this document. There has been some confusion about conflicting available copies of the NISPOM, and the supplemental copy produced in 2004 acknowledges that Chapter 8 on (Information Security) was written in 1998 and as of that date had not been updated. The DoD released a revised version in February of 2006. This is the version used for my purposes here. This chapter is an interpretation of the document and the process. Contractors who live under the N ISP tell me the terms can be interpreted differently on a case by case basis by representatives of the DoD. This chapter then serves as a general overview of the intent and applicability of specific security issues covered in this book and I do not represent this to be an official interpretation of the exact terms a contractor would need to satisfy in order to obtain certification.

Also, any reference to the DoD Orange Book comes with the same caveat. While the Orange Book has been the defacto standard for information security within the DoD, versions that are available to the general public are outdated. Only fully cleared military personnel have access to the official documents. The mention of the Orange Book here is referential only and does not intend to be an official interpretation.

Certification

Section 2 of Chapter 8 of the NISPOM gives a clear picture of what is required to obtain certification. It begins with a clarification that the security measures must be in place and then certified. While there are provisions for certifying subsequent measures that are in progress under the initial certification, the systems must be designed and all security measures in place before the certificate will be issued. There has been some confusion with contractors on this. The operating manual, however, is clear.

The operating manual is also clear the security measures may be tested on site before certification is issued. This helps the certifying body determine if the system is built to accommodate and support an acceptable level of risk. That level of risk is decided by the certifying body, not the contractor. Before any classified information can sit on the server and be accessed by approved contractual personnel, this determination must be made in advance.

There is a provision to grant interim approval, but this is decided by the certifying body and the manual is clear the security measures must be in place for the first 180 days of provisional certification, and then for the possible 180 day extension. The process of reaccreditation must be completed whenever the contractor substantially changes their security processes or upgrades there is infrastructure. The IS Security Manager (ISSM) determines if the changes warrant a review by the certifying body and they are soley responsible for determining if reaccreditation is necessary.

The certifying bidy can revoke the certificate if specific security measures are removed, fail or are altered so as to not provide the acceptable level of risk. The system is then sanitized and all classified information is removed.

In the event the contractor wishes to certify multiple systems, they are required to submit a Master System Security Plan (Master SSP). Once the first system is certified under the plan, all subsequent systems are certified only when they meet the acceptable level of risk. A through risk assessment is conducted by the certifying body with the assistance of approved contractor personnel.

Common Requirements

Section 3 of Chapter 8 lists of the requirements for securing systems is lengthy and comprehensive. The reader will identify the topics covered in this book.

1) Cleaning and Sanitizing
2) Examination of Hardware and Software
3) Identification and Authentication
4) Maintenance
5) Malicious Code
6) Marking Hardware, Output and Media
7) Physical Security
8) Protection of Media
9) Review of Output and Media
10) Configuration Management

Clearing and Sanitizing

The intent of this section is to either totally remove classified information from a system, such as in the case of loss of certification, or to reuse the media. In the case of media re-use, it is cleared to prevent access to the information that was stored there. Sanitizing is a lower level of data removal. The specific guidelines for clearing and sanitizing are the province of the certifying body and issued to the contractor.

Examination of Software and Hardware

The certifying body will examine all commercial or proprietary software to ascertain if there are bugs, viruses, incompatibilities or anything else that might be considered detrimental to the security of the classified information.

Hardware is also examined to ensure it is in good working order and does not present a security risk.

Identification and Authentication Management

This is for obvious reasons one of the most extensively detailed parts of the chapter covering IS security. How people log n, how their user profiles are managed, the development of passwords, the removal of users and the re-use of log in IDs are meticulously covered. The chapters in authentication, password management and access controls in this book are a good guideline for meeting these standards. Of particular interest in this section is the standard for password generation and management. The certifying body will define how passwords are generated and where they are stored. Writing them down on a sticky note and placing them under the keyboard is absolutely not acceptable.

Maintenance

The NISPOM recognizes my long held belief that a system is extremely vulnerable during both routine and unscheduled maintenance. There are two tiers of personnel allowed to conduct maintenance; Cleared and Uncleared. Cleared personnel do not require an escort, but uncleared personnel not only require appropriately cleared personnel to escort them, but they will also be subject to keystroke monitoring. Uncleaared personnel will not have any access to classified data even while being escorted and monitored. Their role is hardware maintenance only.

Malicious Code

The standard established in earlier chapters of this book are to be met in regards to constantly monitoring for any malicious codes and the download of necessary security patches to the operating system.

Physical Security

The standard here is not only the use of locks and cameras to observe the physical space, but the uses of access logs to data bases and security devices placed on hardware. The hardware will also be supported with alternate power supplies and surge/suppress protection to ensure the integrity and availability of the data on the hardware.

Review of Output and Media

The classified information stored on the system is to remain classified even when hard copy or electronic copy stored on portable media is required. The certifying body will determine all necessary clearance procedures for the production and distribution of the information that passes from the information system to an area outside of the protected zone.

Configuration Management

The intent here has been thoroughly covered in this book; assess and catalogue all hardware and software, determine reliability of connectivity, determine the sensitivity of ports and hardware and then document this in a Configuration Management Plan.

Protection Measures

Section 4 of chapter 8 defines levels of protection measures for varying types of data. The matrices in this section define sensitivity for the Confidentiality, Integrity and Availability of data. The three levels are High, Medium and Basic for each. Confidential information can be Top Secret and Secret, or Secret and Secret Restricted and then simply

Confidential. For the Integrity of the data, the three levels are absolute accuracy, high degree of accuracy and then a reasonable degree of accuracy. The Availability of data is determined by Immediately Available On Demand, Readily Available, and then Available with a flexible tolerance for delay.

Theses standards are then tested against clearance matrices and then against the various standards of the operating manual. Once these matrices are understood, it becomes clear that the operating manual sets a clear standard for protecting classified information but also allows for normal operations for lower or non-classified data. One former contractor complained his operations were unduly restricted by the standards in the operating manual, but he also admitted he tried to secure everything and did not utilize the lower levels of acceptable Confidentiality, Integrity and Availability allowed.

Protection Requirements

Section 6 of Chapter 8 defines protection requirements. This includes alternate power supplies, auditing capability, backup and restoration procedures, changes to data that affect integrity, data transmission, access controls, identification and authentication, separation of functions, system recovery and disaster recovery planning.

The National Industrial Security Program Operating Manual is based on solid, proven security measures that should apply to any sensitive data. While the research and development of the tools necessary for national security are extremely important, so is data pertaining to the finances and trade secrets of corporations and my personal data.

Beginning with a basic understanding of networking and the transmission of data, we have carefully followed these rigid standards throughout this book and seen how these standards are necessary for securing these types of data.

The sad reality is that outside of contractors working on national security, too many people fail to educate themselves on these issues and how simple they are to implement. Therefore, sensitive data goes unprotected. Fortunately, lawmakers are catching up with laws governing the security of financial, health and personal data.

Conclusion

As I was writing this book, I consulted with several people who manage small to medium sized companies who are entirely dependent on their information systems. And while their computer provide the lifeline to their customers, suppliers, employees and perhaps even financial resources, most of these people said they had never considered the importance of the issues in this book. They were happy with some virus protection and they called it good.

Not even the events of 9/11 woke them up enough to take network security seriously. They all admitted had I not asked their opinion of the work, much of what they read would not have seemed important, that is until their computer networks went down.

I was associated with a private post secondary educational institution prior to taking on my present position at San Diego State University. The person responsible for assisting graduates of that institution in their efforts to find work in the area of their studies lamented the stagnation of salaries for entry to mid level network engineers and information security specialists. Also, instead of hiring network support personnel or even out sourcing on site network support, a few of them designated someone within the organization in this position without any formal education in network engineering. Managers have decided to cut spending on network support and most of the people I spoke to in this process spent little or nothing on network security.

A business contracting with the Department of Defense as we saw in this book is required to secure their systems and data to a very high standard. Small companies not associated with government work are not. The suppliers of the contractors, if they do not handle defense secrets are not required to secure their systems.

I am not normally an alarmist. I have tried to approach the topic of network security in a logical and rational method without causing undue fear. However, after speaking with several owners and managers I was made acutely aware that most systems are not secure. One fairly large organization I visited has more than one thousand employees. There is a network administrator on staff. However, when I asked for a tour of the facility I saw perhaps three hundred of the workstations. Passwords were taped on monitors, systems were logged on to financial data and the chair was empty and when we got to the server room in the basement, the server room was propped open to cool it off. The administrator admitted he spent little or no time in the room and was not even aware the light bulb was out. I asked him about back ups and he laughed. He was allowed to buy one tape and he was required to reuse it every week.

I was chatting with a Chief Security Officer of a small, regional bank. He said the employees frequented the same small restaurant that shared the strip mall with the bank. One day, the employees found a basket of flash storage devices all shaped like snowboards with the name of a charitable organization printed on them. The sign on the basket said "Free; take one" and most of the employees did. Within a few hours upon their return from lunch as they plugged the devices into USB ports, they noticed their entire database of customer data had been compromised. The virus simply copied all data bases and sent them to a now non-existent email address. And, yes, the charitable organization was also bogus.

A family owned financial services firm controlling several hundred millions of dollars in assets out sourced their network support to a company who also managed the network for their rival service firm. The animosity between the two firms was notorious, and the smaller rival paid the network administrator to copy client data. This was a crime easily detected and multiple persons were charged. However, preventing this was probably even easier and the owner of the larger firm admitted he never considered how risky it was to have allowed the situation to exist.

A privately owned chain hotel offered free wireless connections to their clientele. They had a user interface that required guests to enter a user name and password. It was the same user name and password for every guest. They figured the guests were transitory enough they would not be a local threat once their business in town was done. A student who frequented the bar in the hotel overheard a conversation between a guest and a staff member of the hotel about this and was able to capture the wireless service from his apartment building down the street. He quickly figured out the IP addressing sequence, found the IP address for the managed router and was able to gain administrative access to the router using the same username and password the guests used. He literally then was in control of the entire wireless network and potentially the laptop computers using the system. The flawed security was discovered during an audit of the hotel and instead of filing charges, the hotel just let the matter drop rather than suffer the embarrassment and potential loss of business.

It is not an exaggeration to state that the most vulnerable aspect of our society today is the computer networks managing our money, supplies, customer data and personal information. The laws are tough and anyone who is successfully tried for cracking a computer is dealt with severely, but most systems are vulnerable because so little attention is paid the security basics contained in this book. Even worse, some companies will not press charges for fear of losing business.

Securing a network is a lot of work, but it is necessary. Hopefully this book has awakened you to the need to focus on network security and also that a solid network security policy and its implementation is not rocket science.

Glossary

Circuit Flap - A condition where connectivity is disrupted when the circuits carrying data are not sufficient for the amount of data.

CISSP - Acronym for the Certified Information Systems Security Professional certification offered by (ISC)2

Cracker - A person who writes malicious code such as viruses and spybots and also intentionally disrupts networking services or destroys hardware and data.

Demarcation - The point the local service providers for telephone, cable and fiber optic lines enter the building and truncate the external access lines.

DHCP - Dynamic Host Control Protocol provides the Internet Protocol address to the computers on a network.

Encryption - A method of securing data by systematically replacing letters with other letters, numbers and symbols using specific algorithms called keys. The key that creates the encryption algorithm is used to decrypt the data, replacing it to its original form.

Extranet - A shared access resource usually intended for limited access. The extranet is normally used for hosting corporate websites that only employees can access for training, employee handbooks and the like.

H.323 - A communications protocol used in such applications as Instant Messaging.

Infrastructure - The wired connections of any size network, including the demarcation point to the wall jack and all distribution hardware in the system.

Internet Service Provider - A reseller of access to the World Wide Web.

IP - Internet Protocol; acronym for the protocol used for addressing computers on a network.

Local Area Network - (LAN) A small to medium sized network used within a home, small business that does not typically span between buildings, cities or states.

MAC - Media Access Control; A number that is unique to the device connecting the computer to a network, typically found in the Network Interface Card (NIC).

Metropolitan Area Network - (MAN) A network spanning across several locations in one metropolitan area.

MPLS - Multi Protocol Label Switching; A technology used to transfer data through a switch rather than a router.

Node - A device conneted to a network that ultizes or offers networked services such as a server, router, workstation, printer.

Quality of Service - This is measured two ways and both are equally important. 1) The guarantee of a connection when it is needed and 2) the integrity of the queuing of data that must be sent at a specific time.

Rootkits - A software program that attacks the root of the computer. The most typical manifestation of the existence of a rootkit is when processes and programs running on a computer are concealed and cannot be seen by anyone except the owner/writer of the rootkit.

Spyware - A computer program placed on a hard drive that tracks what a person does on the computer including the web sites visited and can be sophisticated enough to log or track every keystroke entered into the keyboard.

SSID - Service Set Identifier is the name given to the wireless network. This is normally set in a configurable wireless router or access point.

Storage Area Network - (SAN) A group or cluster of computers specifically designated for data storage.

T-1 - A commercial level service access able to carry 1.54 Mbits per second.

Viritual Private Network - A connection between two nodes of a computer, typically from a remote location, that is secured in various ways. This allows remote users to access the network resources from hotels, home and even motorhomes.

Wide Area Network - (WAN) A computer network spanning multiple cities, states or countries.

WiFi - Wireless Fideltiy is a protocol for transmitting data from one access point to another, typically directly to the wireless NIC in the computer.

WPA - WiFi Protected Access is an encryption standard for limiting access to a wireless network.

Index

B

C

I

L

M

N

O

P

Q

R

S

T

U

V

W